THE

HISTORY AND GOVERNMENT

OF

NEBRASKA.

By JAY AMOS BARRETT, M.A.,

INSTRUCTOR IN GREEK AND CIVICS, LINCOLN HIGH SCHOOL, 1889-1892;
AND AUTHOR OF "THE EVOLUTION OF THE
ORDINANCE OF 1787."

LINCOLN, NEB.:
J. H. MILLER, PUBLISHER.
1892.

LINCOLN, NEB:
PACE, WILLIAMS & NORTH,
PRINTERS,

To

My Parents,

In Recognition of their Devotion to Family, Loyalty to
Country, and Thorough Integrity
in All Things,

This Book

is

Affectionately Dedicated.

CONTENTS.

PART I.—HISTORY.

PART II.—CIVIL GOVERNMENT.

MAPS.

PREFACE.

The annals of Nebraska are so little known and the place of a citizen is so faintly comprehended, that no apology is necessary for offering this volume to the teachers and scholars of the State. A man cannot know his duty to his neighbor or to his government unless he understands how he is related to the other members of society. This work is offered in the hope that it may be easier for teachers to create an interest in this line of study, and also that the work may be useful in private study.

I desire to thank the several friends that have helped me in preparing this book, especially Mr. Frank E. Bishop and Mr. George W. Woodbury. To Prof. George E. Howard I am indebted for my interest in historical work, and I wish to publicly express my appreciation of his fidelity as a teacher.

JAY A. BARRETT,

LINCOLN, August 22, 1892.

INTRODUCTION.

The American people are but just beginning to realize the importance of the study of history; especially of their own history, and more especially of local history. Indeed, the latter has long been in the condition of the prophet who is always without honor in his own country. Men have travelled many weary miles, and have expended large sums of money and hours of valuable time, to learn that which has lain at the door of some really intelligent citizen without his ever recognizing that it was or could be of value or interest to himself or to others. The history of some other state, or county, or town—of some other people—that is grand and stirring, and its perusal is fraught with inspiration, with warning, with instruction, with reproof. But we have lived such monotonous lives, we have always been such common people, there has been so little that has been at all striking or out of the usual run of things; of what earthly value or interest are our simple chronicles? Great men and great events are like the ague—always in the next county.

But the time has come when we begin to recognize that this country of ours has been made what it is, not by so-called leaders, or by speech-makers, or by any imposing figures on the canvass, but by very common people indeed. We have advanced, not by startling leaps and rapid bounds, but by painful and continuous effort, and by this effort on the part of all the people. And we have come to understand that this progress of the people and of the whole people is of more value and of more interest than the pedigree of kings; no matter what kind of kings they may be. The mad career of robber Rome, the rush of mailed knights, the battles of kingdoms for existence—in order that they might the more successfully prey upon each other; this is or at least has been very taking, and has been on the tongues' end of all our children. But now we ask more about the white-wained prairie schooners, the little settlements that gradually encroach upon the desert or the wilderness; the men and women who made homes in the sod houses and the dugouts, and the simple folk that while laboring for their daily bread created magnificent mediterranean republics in this but recently an unknown land.

He who calls attention to the beginnings of things in this spirit of thankfulness for the work that was thus done and thus well done, who is willing to embalm the more simple story of early struggles for a free state, who calls attention to our own ancestry and our own past, he is worthy of both recognition and gratitude. Mr. Barrett has done this and more in the little volume for which he has very courteously asked me to write the introduction. Faithfully and patiently he has threaded together the events of early Nebraska life, and has put the result within the reach of every child in the State. The little volume is intended primarily for use in the schools, and that is exactly where it ought to be placed. In the hands of a good teacher, and there should be no others, it will go very far towards giving a correct perspective of our history, towards placing things in their true light and true relations. That the narrative is correctly given is vouched for by the training of the author, received at that University which this State has wisely placed at the head of its system of free schools, and by the excellent work which he has done in other lines and which has received due and prompt recognition by those amply able to speak with authority in such matters.

In adding the chapters on Local Government, the author has greatly increased the value of the volume. Many a man knows all about how the national government is and should be regulated, but cannot name the more simple duties and responsibilities of a probate judge. Many a man can discuss the tariff very learnedly, but has very little idea about local taxation. But the fact is that the home government demands our first attention and our greatest care. That touches us more closely than any other form of public life or organization. Only as the local work is well done and intelligently done, can we hope that the government of the nation will be what it ought to be.

The references to some of the more elementary authorities in the volume lead naturally to the remark, which cannot be out of place here, that there ought to be in every common school in the State a good library, which shall be at the same time a circulating library for the families of the district. A small sum intelligently expended each year would soon work wonders. It is not difficult to see how even this slight addition to the amount now raised, would in some districts, because of our wretchedly unequal method of taxation, seem unbearable. But the good sense of the people of this State will not long endure such a system as is now in vogue. When a county tax is substituted for the present inefficient and unnecessarily burdensome system, the school library will be within easy reach.

No lover of Nebraska, and no one desiring to see better citizenship in this State, can fail to welcome as earnest and painstaking and successful an effort as is this little volume.

JAMES H. CANFIELD.

LINCOLN, August 15, 1892.

PART I.
History of Nebraska.

HISTORY OF NEBRASKA.

I.—PHYSICAL FEATURES.

The location of a city or state has much to do with the amount of its rainfall, the strength of its winds and the severity of its weather. It is not enough, therefore, to say that the piece of country called Nebraska lies slightly north of the center of the United States. More than that, it lies on the western side of the great valley drained by the Missouri and Mississippi rivers, bordering on the **SITUA-** former. It stretches from that muddy **TION.** river on the east to the foothills of the Rocky Mountains on the west. The presence of this high range between Nebraska and the Pacific Ocean keeps out winds and moisture from that direction. Its situation, also, with regard to the large body of water south of it must not be overlooked. The Gulf does not seem to be near enough to affect Nebraska much, yet it has a very important influence upon the climate. Only level country intervenes between this state and the water to the south.

In size Nebraska is much larger than the average state. If all divisions of the United States were made the same in size, each would be about 63,000 square miles in extent. Nebraska has 76,885 square miles. Such large figures, however, do not give much idea of its vastness. South Dakota has almost exactly the same area, but Kansas, Utah and Minnesota are somewhat larger, each having over 80,000 square miles. How many of the eastern states could be comfortably located in one of these ordinary western common-wealths like Nebraska or Kansas? From their areas, it appears that all the New England states, **SIZE.** with Delaware and New Jersey besides, have about 72,000 square miles. How do these divisions of the western prairies, of which there are so many that they seem very ordinary to Americans, compare with European countries? The larger areas of that continent are, of course, very much greater in extent. Austria, the German Empire, or France, is about three times the size of Nebraska. Spain, Turkey, Sweden, Norway and Italy are each more exten-sive. But with the smaller areas, most of the republics contained in the Union compare very favorably. Greece with all its islands, Denmark, Switzerland, Belgium, Holland and Wales are to-gether about equal to Nebraska in size.

The northern and southern boundaries of the State are formed, for the most part, by the paral-lels of 40° and 43°. The Missouri, flowing south-east, is the eastern boundary between these lines. The place where this river crosses the northern parallel is about twenty-one and one-half degrees west of Washington, and at the southeastern corner of the State the river is eighteen and one-half degrees. Therefore the Missouri, as a boundary of the State, flows eastward about 170 miles and **BOUND-** southward over 200. The parallel of 40° **ARIES.** is the southern boundary only as far west as the 25th meridian from Washington. The line then follows this meridian to the parallel of 41° which forms the remainder of the southern boundary, thus leaving a large rectangular area out of the southwestern corner. The western limit is the 27th meridian. The longest distance across the State from east to west is about 420 miles. From north to south, about 208. The longest distance within the limits, from southeast to northwest, is over 500 miles.

Nebraska is distant nearly 850 miles in a direct line from the mouth of the Mississippi river. The descent from the upper valleys averages only one foot to the mile, making the southeastern corner of the State somewhat less than 875 feet above the Gulf. Starting from this lowest land, the rise is both north and west. At Omaha, which is about **ELEVA-** one hundred miles north in a direct line, **TION** the surface is a hundred feet higher, and **AND** **SLOPE.** at Covington, another hundred miles further north, the river varies between 1,076 and 1,100 feet. The land all along the eastern border lies high above the level of the river, in bluffs and steep ascents. Along the southern boundary the rise is more rapid. From the general level of the southeastern county, beginning at 900 feet, the

country attains an elevation of 3,258 feet at
Haigler, in the southwestern corner. This distance is about 360 miles, and the rise is therefore
about six and one-half feet to the mile. This
rise is quite gradual the whole distance, but a
little more rapid in the western part. Similarly
the Platte valley descends from 4,096 feet at Sid-
ney to 950 feet at its mouth. From Ponca, in the

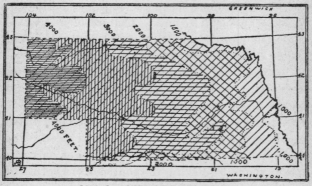

MAP I. LINES OF ELEVATION.

(After Henry Gannett, 1880. Ho. Misc. Doc., 47th Cong., 2nd Sess.,Vol.
13. Map 19. Washington, 1883.)

northeastern corner, which is 1,141 feet, the State
rises to 3,628 feet at Mansfield, in the extreme
northwest. Across the State, from north to south,
there does not seem to be great difference between
the elevations of the river valleys and of the land
which separates them. Four valleys show the
following altitudes a little west of center of the
State:

The Republican, at Culbertson, 2,565 feet.

The Platte, at North Platte, 2,804 feet.

The Middle Loup, at Thedford, 2,842 feet.

The Niobrara, at Valentine, 2,579 feet.

It would seem from these that the center of the State is higher than the northern and southern borders, and that the Niobrara and the Republican rivers are of about the same height above the Gulf. The highest points in the State are in the extreme west. The map shows that the land all along the western boundary is above 4,000 feet. Scott's Bluff is thought to be the highest point in the State and is given at nearly 6,000 feet, while Pine Ridge lacks only 500 feet of this.

Nebraska is very well situated in respect to drainage, and is well supplied with rivers and creeks. The smooth and gently sloping surface has a tendency to distribute the running water evenly over the surface of the country. There are three separate valleys of considerable size. In the center of the State and running the whole length from west to east is the Platte River. Its valley occupies very nearly half the State. Most of its tributaries are on the north side, because the water-shed which separates it from the Republican Valley on the south is close to it. It drains the country much more than half way to the Niobrara on the north. The names *Platte* and *Nebraska* are the same in meaning, the first being **DRAIN-** French and the latter Indian. They sig- **AGE.** nify *shallow water*. Extending almost the whole length of the northern border is the valley of the Niobrara, which is said to be a Ponca

word meaning the same as the word *Nebraska*.
This river drains about a sixth of the State. The
Republican River, which courses half the length
of the southern boundary and then turns south
into Kansas, receives the water from a larger part
of the State than the Niobrara by about 2,000
square miles. In the northeast and southeast,

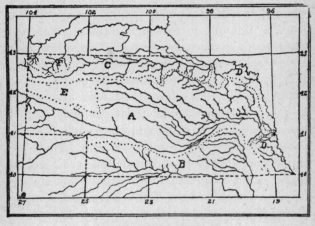

MAP II. RIVER SYSTEMS.

A. Valley of the Platte.
B. Valley of the Repub ican.
C. Valley of the Niobrara.
D. Lands draining directly into the Missouri.
E. Lands without surface drainage.
F. Lands drained by the Cheyenne and White rivers.

small areas drain directly into the Missouri. In
the northwestern part is a triangular piece of
country that does not appear to have any connection with the large rivers that drain the State, at
least on the surface. There are some small creeks
which run a few miles and then are entirely taken

into the soil again. This tract occupies upward of 7,000 square miles.

The mean annual temperature of the State varies from 46° to 51°. As in the case of the rainfall, it is highest in the southeast. **CLIMATE.** During the spring and summer there are many consecutive days with the temperature above 50°, and this fact is of great importance to the farmers. The highest temperatures that occur anywhere in North America are found within a tract of country extending the full length of the Missouri and Mississippi rivers, **TEM-PERA-TURE.** and lying for the most part west of them. The central and southeastern parts of Nebraska lie in this region. It is expected that at times the mercury will reach a high figure. The greatest recorded temperature of the State is 112° above zero, and the lowest 35° below. There is therefore a range of 147°.

Temperature and rainfall in Nebraska seem to be arranged so that the farmer may get the largest amount of good at the growing season. The annual fall of rain is twenty-four inches, a very ordinary amount compared with other places further east. If this were evenly distributed throughout the year, there would be for each month only two inches of rain. This would not be enough to allow the crops usually planted in the State to mature properly. Fortunately it is not so distributed, for much of it comes just when the growing and maturing crops need it. About two-thirds of all the rain falls during the five months from April to August inclusive. In the winter months, when there is less need for rain, very little falls. For each of the months of November, December, January **RAIN-** uary and February, the average is less **FALL.** than an inch. In comparison with the states directly east of it, Nebraska has not so large an annual fall of rain, but the country is as favorably situated for agriculture, because that which does fall comes when it does the most good. In its distribution over the State, the southeast is more fortunate than the west. The rainfall in the former is even greater than in the extreme eastern states, from Maine to Virginia. The amount gradually decreases toward the western and northwestern regions of the State, where the average for the year is smaller than in the eastern half of the United States. It is often insufficient to produce good crops. The weather reports fail to show that there is any increase in the rainfall, yet there is a general impression that the amount is greater than it was many years ago.

West of the Mississippi, from the Gulf to British America, is an uninterrupted plain, sloping gradually from north to south. A former Chief Signal Officer of the United States, Gen. A. W. Greeley, says that there is here, perhaps, the most remarkable wind system in the world.[1] The winds blow continuously and often violently over these plains, because they are so extensive and

---

[1] *American Weather,* 172.

almost no obstructions exist. In general, the winds are strongest near the sea, and their force grows less and less towards the interior of a country. But here is found a notable exception.

WINDS. Here the winds are as strong as near the coast and are often more violent. In a country heated as readily by the sun as these plains are, there will be occasional breezes from every quarter. But the surroundings of the region give the prevailing direction to the winds. One expects to find them blowing mostly from the north or from the south, because the great Rocky Mountain Range extends all along the west. The weather reports show that this is true. During the year 1890, more than half of the monthly reports from weather stations in Nebraska gave prevailing north and northwest winds. A smaller number of reports showed winds from the very opposite direction. There was scarcely any east wind, and comparatively few times did west and southwest winds prevail. The wind in Nebraska most frequently blows in the same direction in which the Rocky Mountains and the Missouri river extend. In the year mentioned, north and northwest winds prevailed during the eight months from October to May inclusive. For the four other months of the year, the winds were from the south and southeast.

Among the things which visitors remember longest after passing a winter or a summer in the State of Nebraska, are the storms. Especially is this true of the winter storm called a blizzard,

STORMS which occurs here quite as frequently as in Dakota or Minnesota. The disturbances of the atmosphere called by the Weather Bureau "*low area storms*" and "*high area storms*," usually start on the eastern slopes of the Rocky Mountains, either at the northwest near the headwaters of the Missouri, or at the southwest in New Mexico. If they start in the northwest, they generally take one of two directions: either they pass eastward over the Great Lakes,

(a) **Low Area Storms.** or else they go southeast, following the Missouri valley. In the latter case the storm is felt in Nebraska, but commonly passes too far to the north to affect the State seriously. When currents of air over a large extent of territory move towards the center, going round in the direction opposite to a clock's motion as they come together, and rising there, the whole is called a cyclonic or low area storm. The center of the disturbance also moves along like the little eddies or whirls of water in the rivers. In the case of a storm such as this, the air is disturbed for hundreds of miles on every side. In any one place the wind blows toward the center of the storm, unless that is near. The general rule is "Turn your back to the wind, and the center of the storm is to your left." It is usually in the southeastern

Tornadoes. part of these low area storms that *tornadoes* occur. These are so-called by the Weather Bureau, but they are known in the news-

papers as cyclones. Nebraska is so situated with
regard to the passage of low area storms, either
from the northwest or from the southwest, as to
escape many that occur to the northeast, east, or
southeast. As storms pass up from the southwest, many tornadoes begin in the eastern part of
Kansas, and go over into Missouri. The loss of
life from tornadoes in the latter state is greater
than anywhere else in the United States.

Winter storms are generally of the other kind.
In these the air moves in the opposite direction in
all respects. It goes away from the center, at
which the air is descending, and circles round in
the same direction as the hands of a clock. Another name for them is *anti-cyclones*. During this
kind of a storm, the cold air pours down from the
north across the smooth plains, often swiftly
and violently. With enough snow to fill the air,
it becomes the *blizzard*. It begins in
(b) **High Area Storms.** the north, above Montana and Dakota,
and either passes directly to the south
across Nebraska and Kansas, or crosses the
country eastward and enters the St. Lawrence
valley. Sometimes it takes a half-way course between these two. The danger from blizzards in the
north lies in the combination of high wind, intense cold, and drifting snow. High area storms
also cause great damage to crops further south,
by carrying snow and cold even into Florida. To
this class belong the great storms of February
9-14, 1881, and January 12, 1888.

There is such an immediate connection between
the agriculture of a state and its geology, that it is
proper to take a glance here at the rocks of Ne-
ROCKS   braska.   In   its youth   the   Earth   was
AND   mostly covered with water.   It has been
SOILS.   found out that the part of North America
which first showed itself, was a V-shaped piece of
land extending northward from the Great Lakes.
Nebraska was still sea-bottom.   The ceaseless
action of the water upon the original rocks constantly formed sediment, and during untold ages
layers were gathering over the surface of the State.
For an inconceivably long time this process went
on, the land-surface slowly increasing and the
water growing more shallow.   The sediment de-
THE   posited by the water became hard, and is
EARLI-   now called limestone, sandstone and shales.
EST
ROCKS.   There finally came a period when the
whole swampy region from Pennsylvania to Nebraska was covered by the rankest growth of
vegetation.   After great masses of plant life had
accumulated, the level of the surface sank, letting
in the salt water again and causing a layer of
sediment over the vegetation.   In this manner the
great coal beds of the country were formed.   The
growth of plant life was not so heavy in the
West as in Pennsylvania and the East, for the
beds of coal that are found in Nebraska are comparatively thin.   This process of forming coal beds
went on until there were in some parts of North
America as many as seventy-six seams of coal with

COAL MEAS- URES. the intervening deposits of rock. All these layers together are called the coal measures. It is only in the southeastern part of Nebraska that these rocks appear. The layers of coal are too thin and the quality too poor for it to be mined, except for local use. Of the limestone, shale and sandstone which make up the sediment deposited at this time, the first is the most important, both for making soil and for building purposes. These oldest rocks on the

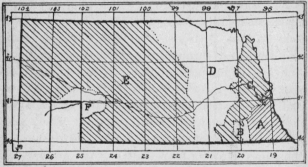

(After a map of Prof. Lewis E. Hicks in *Agricultural Report of Nebraska, 1889*, p 367.)

MAP III. GEOLOGICAL MAP: LAYERS OF ROCK.

A. Coal Measures.	D, F. Colorado Group.
B. Permian.	E. Area of the Lake
C. Dakota Group.	Deposits.

surface of the State cover a little more than six counties in the southeastern corner.

The name *Carboniferous* is applied to the age of coal. The following period the geologists call the *Permian*. Almost all the rocks of this time that appear in Nebraska are in Gage county. They resemble rocks previously made, but are without coal. During the two following periods Nebraska was out of water, and the results are apparent only in the valleys, which were made at that time by the water just about where they are to-day. Then the sea came again at the slow sinking of the land, and the valleys became

THE TWO GROUPS OF THE CRETACEOUS PERIOD. gulfs or bays, into which were brought many kinds of stones, sands, and clays. Such are the shaly and hard sandstones, quartzite, lignite, etc., called altogether the Dakota Group. The surface of the State where this is exposed, is in the northeast, next to the Missouri, extending to the south and southwest through Saunders, Lancaster, Saline and Jefferson counties. Next west of these rocks comes the Colorado Group, in the eastern and northeastern part of the State, with a small area in Cheyenne and Keith counties. The readiness with which these rocks are broken gives them the name of rotten limestone, and the presence of chalk in them in some localities causes them to be called chalk rock. They consist of limestones, shales and clays. All rocks of the cretaceous period were deposited by the sea, and fossils of

THE FRESH-WATER LAKE. marine life occur throughout them. The remaining surface of the State was covered during the next period by a freshwater lake. This left upon its bottom all the kinds of rock that were formed earlier. The layers of each period overlap the earlier layers, with the newest at the West and the earliest at the southeast.

'From rocks comes directly and indirectly the soil that covers them. Air, water, heat and cold, and many other forces besides, act upon the hardest substance, cracking and crumbling it, and finally reducing it to dust. All the rocks laid upon the face of Nebraska ages ago now themselves are covered by this dust, mixed with decayed vegetable and animal life that lived upon it. The deposits on the surface of Nebraska make as fertile soils for the farmer as are known in the world.

SOILS. The special soil of each locality, however, needs to be studied by the one who tills it. The accumulations from the wearing of the rocks receive special names, according to the time or manner in which they came. Thus there is the *glacial drift,* that was scattered over the State by the action of the great ice fields that once lay north of Nebraska. There are also *loess, adobe, alluvium, muck, peat and marl,* each of great value to plant life.

The inhabitants of Nebraska laugh at the old geographies, in which was told a story of the "Great American Desert" west of the Missouri **PLANT LIFE.** River. After James Monroe took his first journey over the Allegheny Mountains into the Ohio valley in 1785, he wrote to Thomas Jefferson as follows: "A great part of the territory is miserably poor, especially that near Lakes Michigan and Erie; and that upon the Mississippi and Illinois consists of extensive plains which have not had, from appearances, and will not have

a single bush on them for ages."[1] The millions
of bushels of grain raised in that region every
year show that Mr. Monroe was very much mistaken, and so were the geographers later, when
THE   they made a guess about the lands be-
IDEA
OF A   tween the Missouri and the Rockies. A
DESERT
party of explorers and scientists, after
spending the winter of 1819–20 a few miles north of
where Omaha now is, followed the Platte River to
the south fork, and turning south made their way
back along the Arkansas River. They thought
that they had "completely established one important fact: that the whole division of North
America drained by the Missouri, the Arkansas
and their tributaries, between the meridian of the
mouth of the Platte and the Rocky Mountains, is
almost entirely unfit for cultivation and therefore
uninhabitable by a people depending upon agriculture for their subsistence."[2]

All the plant life that grows wild in a particular state or country is called its flora. Students
have been diligently at work collecting the different kinds of plant life that grow in Nebraska
and up to 1892 they have found about 2,500 species. When each hill and valley has been
FLORA.
searched, no doubt the number will be
very much larger. Each locality usually has a
variety of plants that have become suited to its
soil, elevation, and climate, or have been brought

---

[1] Bancroft, *History of Formation of Const.*, i., 480–1.

[2] Gov. Black, quoting the published narrative of *Long's Expedition*,
1819, written by Dr. James. *Council Journal, 6th Session, p. 9.*

there by accident. A large state usually has several regions with somewhat different flora. Nebraska has three: the part along the Missouri, **THE THREE RE- GIONS.** the most western portion and the intervening district. In the eastern part is found the kind of plant life that resembles the flora of the Mississippi Valley at the same latitude. In the western part appear species that belong to the Rocky Mountains. The central part of Nebraska is a section of the Great Plains stretching far to the north and to the south, which have their own peculiar set of plants.

Salt and alkali are found at places in the State. This allows the growth of plants not usually found except along the coast of the sea. Such a region is the Salt Basin near Lincoln, the flora of which is very interesting on this account. Another **SPE- CIAL FEA- TURES.** special feature of botanical study in Nebraska is the abundance of native grasses, of which 154 species have been already discovered. The composites, or plants like the sun flower and golden rod, are plentiful, and this state is fairly the home of plants having pods like the pods of peas and beans (Leguminosæ).

There is a question among botanists whether this treeless plain was always so. There are ev- **WERE THERE FOR- ESTS LONG AGO?** idences which seem to tell a story of great forests anciently. If it is true that trees once covered the surface of the state from the mountains to the Missouri, the annual burning off of the grass by the Indians explains

2

why the trees were almost all gone when the settlers entered Nebraska. Now there are no more great prairie fires, and Arbor Day has become a legal holiday in the State. Botanists think, however, that the trees were gradually spreading up the valleys from the east before the farmer came.

The large mammals that have inhabited Nebraska are fast becoming extinct. As late as 1872 a grand duke of Russia came to Nebraska for a buffalo hunt, and a party of government **ANIMAL LIFE.** officials and Indians, led by Buffalo Bill, had a grand chase. In Zoology there is a difference between a bison and a buffalo. The animals hunted in Nebraska were bison, but they are almost always spoken of as buffalo. They roamed over the plains in great droves, and were **BUF- FALO OR BISON.** the chief game of the Indians. They have now disappeared from our limits. Elk, deer, and antelope, were numerous when settlement was begun, but they are now rare. Even many years ago bears seem to have been few. Now they are scarcely heard of. The smaller animals, such as wild cats, wolves, coyotes, and foxes, become fewer with the growth of population, like the buffalo and deer. They are hunted less and escape more easily, so that they remain when the buffalo is gone. A complete study of the small animals like moles, mice, and squirrels, has not been made, so that the whole number of mammals cannot be stated with accuracy.

Of the reptiles in the State probably the serpents have been most carefully studied. Twenty-three species are known, among which **SER-PENTS.** are three kinds of rattlesnakes. None of the others are poisonous.

About four hundred species of birds are found in the State. These include those birds which **BIRDS.** stay here all the time, and those stopping in Nebraska during their yearly migrations. The study of the insects of the State is very interesting because their number is very large. This arises from the favorable position of Nebraska. It holds a midway place in the country, both between the north and the south and between the east and the west. Kinds of insects that appear only in one of these regions are usually found here. Insects are like plants in respect to altitude. Some prefer high places and **IN-SECTS.** some the plains, and on account of the range of elevation a large number of insects find a home in the State. Probably more species of the grasshopper kind are found here than anywhere else in the country. The annals of Nebraska tell of the dreadful "grasshopper year," but the insect that visits the State in swarms is a locust. The year 1874 is popularly known as the grasshopper year, because such large numbers came at that time. In reality, however, some section of the State is visited almost every year by these travelers. A dry country without trees favors them. They stay most

of the time in the high plains at the head waters of the great rivers which rise in the Rocky Moun-
LO-
CUSTS. tains, from parallel 40° far to the north into British America. From this part of the country, which is called their *Permanent Home*, they come out upon the surrounding country in swarms. Their number depends upon the kind of season. As far back as there is record of this country, locusts have visited it, and they will continue to visit Nebraska as long as they multiply rapidly in their dry, treeless homes. When trees have been planted through the West, it is supposed that the locusts will not increase so rapidly, while the insects and birds that are harmful to them will be present in greater numbers than before.

AUTHORITIES AND BOOKS OF REFERENCE.

ELEVATION AND SLOPE—Sources of information are mainly
    (1) Elevations given by Railroads;
    (2) *Bulletin of U. S. Geol. Survey*, No. 76., A Table of
    Elevations.

DRAINAGE—Rand, McNally & Co., *Pocket Map of Nebraska*
    1892.

CLIMATE—
    Monthly and *Annual Reports of the Nebraska Weather
    Service.*

    Daily Bulletins of U. S. Signal Service.
    The Climate of Nebraska (Washington, 1891), Sen. Ex.
    Docs., 1st Sess., 50th Cong., 1889-90.
    Gen. A. W. Greeley, *American Weather.*

ROCKS AND SOIL—
    Annual Reports of Neb. State Board of Agriculture,
    1889: Article by Prof. L. E. Hicks.

    Annual Reports of Neb. State Board of Horticulture,
    1887-88, pp. 123-129.

    Prof. Samuel Aughey, *Physical Geog. and Geol. of Ne-
    braska.*

PLANT LIFE—
> *Annual Reports of the Neb. State Board of Agriculture,*
> especially 1889, 1892.
> *Annual Reports of Neb. State Board of Horticulture,*
> especially 1892.
> Contributions from the Botanical Department of the
> University of Nebraska, New Series, III.

ANIMAL LIFE—
> Prof. Aughey, *Physical Geography of Nebraska.*
> *State Agricultural Reports.*
> *U. S. Entomological Reports,* Articles by Prof. Bruner.

SUGGESTIVE TOPICS AND QUESTIONS.

1. Map out the drainage system of your own county.

2. Where in the State has irrigation been tried, and with what success? *State Horticultural Reports,* 1891, p. 148; 1892, p. 78.

3. Can rainfall be artificially produced? What experiments in Nebraska and what results?

4. For the study of climate, every school should have the U. S. weather bulletins. Undoubtedly they will be sent to high schools asking for them. With the help of Gen. Greeley's book called *American Weather,* the maps afford large room for study of the winds, temperature, and storms of the State and of the neighboring region.

5. What is the significance of the terms "*low area storm*" and "*high area storm?*" See *American Weather,* Chap. XIII.

6. WINDS.—Watch carefully the movements of the clouds during a day or a week, and note the following:

(*a*) The number of different currents blowing at the same time.

(*b*) The direction of each, beginning at the lowest. (Frequently the wind is blowing in different directions at different heights.)

(*c*) The swiftest current.

(*d*) Time of day of the greatest wind on the surface of earth.

7. In the study of storms observe (1) the direction from which they come, and (2) changes in the direction of the wind during the storm. How can the direction of the center of the storm be ascertained from the winds? See *American Weather,* p. 195.

8. SCHOOL COLLECTIONS FOR SCIENTIFIC STUDY.—Students should make collections for their schools in the several lines to which their attention is called, as flora of the county or township, insects, birds, etc. After a beginning is made and a place has been provided to receive specimens, additions are easily made. Very few school boards will refuse to fix a place for specimens. Collections are as necessary to the study of botany, geology, etc., as the library is to the study of history.

II.—THE INDIANS.

When white men first crossed the Missouri, Nebraska was not thickly populated with Indians. The prairies formed an excellent hunting ground, and the few tribes in possession of the

OTOES, MISSOURIS, PAWNEES, OMAHAS. country went from place to place in pursuit of large game like deer and buffalo. Captains Lewis and Clark found the Otoe, Missouri, and Pawnee Indians located on the Platte, the Omaha tribe to the northeast, and the Ponca tribe near the mouth of the Niobrara. These were estimated to be a thousand or fifteen hundred warriors at that time. Treaties were made with them immediately after France ceded the country, as had been done with others farther east. The two explorers just mentioned made peace with the tribes of Indians all along their way, in the expedition of 1804. Early treaties were almost entirely of peace and friend-

TREATIES OF (a) Peace, (b) Commerce, (c) Cessions. ship. During the period up to 1830, trade also was regulated by treaty. Finally the Indians began to give up their lands. Cessions seem to begin about 1830, when a tract was reserved between the Great Nemaha and Little Nemaha rivers, called the "half-breed tract." From this time, by many treaties, more and more of the country was given up to the United States, until at last each tribe

was confined to quite narrow limits, called a *re-
serve* or *reservation.* Not all the Indians now in

**RES-
ERVA-
TIONS.**
the State were originally here, nor are all
the tribes still here that were found when
the United States took possession. Some,
like the Iowa and Winnebago tribes, were brought
from other states to live on land chosen for them
in Nebraska. The Pawnees, whose home was
here, sold their land in 1876 and were removed to
Indian Territory.[1]

The *Lacotas,* called by the whites *Dakotas,*
once possessed all the region west of the Mississippi, north of the Arkansas River, and east of
the Rocky Mountains. This nation of Indians
is more commonly known as the Sioux. Four of

**THE
SIOUX.**
the seven tribes which compose it once occupied Dakota and Minnesota, and are
known as the Santee Sioux. The greatest of the
Sioux Nation is the Teton Tribe, whose territory
was north of the Platte, from the Missouri to the
mountains. The Tetons are made up of seven
families, among them being the Blackfeet, the
Brules, and the Ogallalas.

The most abiding hatred existed between the
Pawnees and the Sioux, who spoke altogether different languages. Great battles were fought

---

[1] The *Report of the Commissioner of Indian Affairs, 1891,* p. 114,
gives the following figures regarding the Indians now within the limits
of Nebraska: the number of acres of undivided land belonging to each
tribe, and not owned by individual Indians: Iowa tribe, 11953; Santee
Sioux, 1131; Omaha, 65191; Sauc and Fox, 8013; Ogallala Sioux, 32000;
Winnebago, 14612. Altogether this amounts to 208 square miles.

before settlers came to disturb them. One
STRUG-GLES OVER HUNT-ING GROUND memorable conflict occurred in the year
1832, in what is now Jefferson County,
near the mouth of the Big Sandy River.
Sixteen thousand warriors took part in the
struggle, which lasted for three days. It is said
that the Sioux lost three thousand men, and that
the Pawnees bought their victory with the lives of
two thousand.[1] The last battle between these
same bands occurred in the autumn of 1873, a
few miles west of the present site of Culbertson,
in Hitchcock County. The Sioux surprised the
Pawnees while the latter were at one of their
annual buffalo hunts, overpowering and defeating
them.[2]

The history of the relation between the Indians
and settlers is one long account of petty troubles.
In early times, before the Civil War began in
1861, there seems to have been no general hostility towards the settlers. Histories of counties
are full of the details of Indian scares and of the
RELA-TION BE-TWEEN INDIAN AND SET-TLER: (a) Before 1860. stealing of cattle and horses, and some
loss of life, too, is recorded. On the
other hand it may be said that the Indians
were ill treated, not by the peaceable set-
tler, but by the rougher class of men who
always stay on the frontier. The Indians
resented any personal injury and took vengeance
upon all white people alike. Considering the sav-

[1] Johnson, *History of Nebraska*, 991, where the tradition of the battle is given on the authority of an old French trader, Mont Crevie.
[2] Johnson, *History of Nebraska*, 967-8.

age nature of the Indians, one might readily expect more deeds of cruelty than there really were. Settlers kept themselves ready to meet such bands of Indians as tried to do any damage. Reports of cattle thieving were sufficient to bring together hundreds of armed men. Punishment was not delayed, and probably this explains, to some extent, the usually good behavior of the savage tribes. A marked change was apparent as soon as the Civil War began. The Indians became more hostile. While it lasted, not only did they attack and murder small parties and raid settlements (b) **During the Civil War.** here and there, but the spirit of enmity caused many bands of savages all through the Northwest to combine in attacking settlements. One of the most notable raids was made August 7, 1864, upon the pioneers of Nebraska. At about the same hour of the day all the homes except two along a route of two hundred miles were surrounded and burned. The inmates who could not escape were killed, and their provisions and goods were carried off. The outbreaks did not cease when peace came, although the unusual hostility of the Indians during the war was generally attributed to the influence of white men who favored the South. A writer says that in the neighborhood of Lincoln County the attacks of Indians continued for five years. Since Nebraska became a state comparatively little trouble has arisen, because the limits of their reservations have become too narrow, and the Indians themselves have improved. Even up to a very recent date, however, Indian outbreaks have annoyed the northwestern frontier. The so-called Indian War of 1890-91, like almost all the previ-

"**WAR OF 1890-1891.**" ous conflicts with Indians, began by the failure of the United States to keep its promises. The starving condition of the Indians was only aggravated by the blunders of agents who did not understand how to deal with them. The fighting that occurred may be truly said to have been due to the policy of the government.[1]

AUTHORITIES ON II.

Neb. *State Hist. Soc. Pub.*, especially I., 47–49, 73–85; II., 133–166, 246–48; III., 125–190, 279–286; IV., 30–50, 134–140, 160–191, 281–283.

On Indian Treaties, *U. S. Statutes at Large*, VII. (Indian Treaties); IX., 949; X., 1038, 1043; XI., 729; XIV., 667, 675; XIX., 29, 192, 287, etc.

Johnson's *History of Nebraska*, 55–57, and at various places. This book contains an immense amount of valuable history. Some of the county histories in it are based on the personal knowledge of the writers. It must not be depended on altogether, because it is frequently inaccurate.

Mrs. Helen Hunt Jackson, *A Century of Dishonor*, Chap. V., The Sioux; Chap. VI., The Poncas; Chap. VII., The Winnebagoes.

On classification, see *No. Amer. Rev.*, 110: 45, 55, and General Colby in *State Hist. Soc. Pub.*, III., 144–5.

SUGGESTIVE TOPICS AND QUESTIONS.

1. Is the government justified in its method of making treaties with the Indians?
2. Is the plan of reservations successful?

[1] Further reading upon the history of special tribes and upon the relation between the government and the Indians may be made in Mrs. Jackson's "*A Century of Dishonor.*"

III.—EXPLORERS, MISSIONARIES, AND TRADERS.

The story of the coming of white men into the valleys where our state now is, begins far back before the times which are usually associated with Plymouth Rock and Pocahontas. There is even more romance about the expeditions of the **ANTIQ-UITY OF OUR HIS-TORY.** Spaniards from Mexico and the South into the unexplored interior of the western country than there is about the landing of the pilgrim fathers, or about the planting of a colony at Jamestown. The Spaniards lived in romance. It adds no real dignity to the history of the states that now occupy these prairie lands, to know that it begins as far back as 1541, when Coronado, a Spanish cavalier, came up across the country from the southwest with a **CORO-NADO.** large body of men; still there is a poetry about such a beginning that makes it attractive. After the conquest of Mexico by Cortez, beginning about 1520, that country was ruled by governors. As fast as the natives were conquered, new districts were formed and governors appointed to rule them. In the western part of Mexico was a province called Nueva Galicia over which Coronado was appointed provincial governor in 1538. About that time story was told the Spaniards of seven cities of Cibola to

the north, in which there were immense treas-
THE SEVEN CITIES OF CIBOLA. ures of silver and gold. Coronado was greatly charmed by the prospect of obtaining vast riches by conquest of these cities, and fitted out an expedition. The place was found in the summer of 1541, far north of Mexico. Most historians think that the present town of Zuni stands upon the spot. Although Coronado was disappointed in regard to the gold, he went further, to find the land of the Quivera, where also there was untold wealth to be had. It is
THE LAND OF THE QUIVERA. not certain just what the route of the Spaniards was after they left the seven cities. By the accounts it is certain that Coronado went east and northeast. It is said that he reached the fortieth degree of north latitude. If he did, he and his companions actually set foot on the soil of Nebraska. But he might
DID HE REACH NEBRASKA? easily have been mistaken in supposing that he came as far north as the southern boundary of Nebraska. It is sure, at any rate, that he visited the plains on which the two states of Kansas and Nebraska lie. Whether he really came within the limits of this State is not so important after all. The great fact is that this marks the beginning of the history of white men on these plains. This was. the same year that De Soto was wandering from Florida across the southern slopes to the Mississippi. Henry III. was then King of England; Francis I. held the throne of France, Charles V. was plotting

in the east, and Paul III. was Pope at Rome.
WHAT WAS THE REST OF THE WORLD DOING? Europe as a whole was in the midst of The Reformation, and Luther had shortly before finished his work. The story of the hills and valleys of Nebraska before the time of Coronado must be told by the rocks and revealed by the traditions of the Red Man.

A Spanish expedition about 1601, of which there is a record, took the same general direction as Coronado's. There is also an account of a third, made by the Count of Penelosa in 1662, but strong reasons are found for believing that this one was merely one of the stories that the Count told over **OTHER EXPLORATIONS: SPANISH AND FRENCH** in Spain. In 1673 Father Marquette floated down the Mississippi and learned from the natives about the Missouri and about the Platte. He recorded these rivers on a map just as they were told to him, and this drawing is still preserved. Probably this is the first map of the region. In 1719 Dustine came across the country from the southeast and met the tribes of Indians in the eastern part of Kansas. This is significant of the coming of the French into the plains west of the Missouri and Mississippi. Twenty years after Dustine, two brothers by the name of Mallet came into the country north of the Platte, and explored the river as far west as the Forks.

The history of fur trading in the northwest deals first with the French. In the great center of fur trade, Wisconsin, trading began as early as 1634. After England obtained possession

FUR TRADE: of Canada, the period of French trade

(a) French, 1634-1763. was followed by many years of British traffic. This period may be said to

(b) British, 1763-1816. begin in 1763 and end in 1816, when Congress passed a law prohibiting foreigners from trading within the limits of the United States. The Americans began to compete with the English very early, but the formation of the large companies of the United States

(c) American, 1816-34. begins in 1809, when John Jacob Astor had the American Fur Company chartered. In 1810 two expeditions were started out, one by way of the Missouri River. This year saw a post established at Bellevue. Long before this, however, traders had kept their places of barter on the banks of the Missouri and received the deer and buffalo skins from the Indians. American explorers found traders on Nebraska soil soon after the opening of this century. The annual value of the fur business was very great. During the forty years up to 1847, the annual value to St. Louis is said to have been from two to three hundred thousand dollars.

The expedition made for the government by Lewis and Clark, starting out in 1804, marks the

AMERICAN PATHFINDERS. time when the growing power of the great American Republic began to reach out to these plains. Following this were the undertakings of Major Long in 1819, W. H. Ashley in 1822, Rev. Samuel Parker in 1835, and the well-known expedition of the government under the command of Gen. Fremont in 1842.

By such means as these, information came to the cities and towns of the east, and there began to be an increasing tide of people westward. Traders continued to come to get furs from the Indians, the hunters came for buffalo robes, missionaries came to bring the Gospel to the Indians, and finally the adventurer came to make his fortune. The missionaries separated, some **MIS-SION-ARIES**. going to one tribe and some to another. One of the very earliest within our borders was Moses Merrill, who lived and preached among the Otoes from 1833 to 1840.[1]

Following him were many who went to the various tribes to teach them. Great honor is due the men and women who do this work of self-sacrifice in the early history of any country.

AUTHORITIES AND BOOKS OF REFERENCE.

1. Coronado's Expedition.
   H. H. Bancroft's Works, Vols. XVII. and XXVII.: *Arizona and New Mexico*, pp. 33–72, *History of the Northwest Coast*, I., 44–46. In the former a long list of books concerning the subject is given in note 17, p. 37.
   Gen. J. H. Simpson, in *Smithsonian Reports*, 309–340.
   Judge Savage, in *State Hist. Soc. Pub.*, I., 180–202.
   Magazine of Amer. Hist., XXIII., 288.
   Johnson, *Hist. of Nebraska*, 33–38.
2. Other early explorations.
   State Hist. Soc. Pub., II., 114–131; III., 67–73.
   Bancroft, *Arizona and New Mexico*, 169.
   Hale, *Kansas and Nebraska* (Boston, 1854), 15, 16.
   Winsor, *Narr. and Crit. Hist. of Amer.*, V., 55, note 2.
   Johnson, *Hist. of Nebr.*, 43.

---

[1] The diary of Mr. Merrill is found in the *State Historical Society Publications*, IV., 160–191.

3. American Explorations.
   Lewis and Clark's Travels, (London, 1815, 3 Vols.) I., 35–65.
   Johnson, *Hist. of Nebr.,* 46–55.
   Journal of an Exploring Tour, by Rev. Samuel Parker, (Ithaca, 1842), 39–68.
   Fremont, *Report of the Exploring Expedition* (Washington, 1845), 15–22.
4. Fur Trading.
   F. J. Turner, *Character and Influence of the Fur Trade in Wisconsin, Wis. Hist. Soc. Pub.,* 1889.
   Washington Irving's Works: *Astoria,* Chaps. I.–III., XIII.–XVII. *Bonneville's Adventures,* Chaps. II.–IV.
   Encyclopædias, under names *John Jacob Astor, Fur Trade,* etc.
   Johnson, *Hist. of Nebr.,* 98, 1361, etc.
   Mag. of Amer. Hist., XII., 509.
5. Missionaries.
   State Hist. Soc. Pub., II., 133–166; III., 125–143; IV., 157–191.
   Johnson, *Hist. of Nebr.,* 98, 1363, etc.

IV.—ADVANCE MOVEMENTS.

Two very interesting things happened when the valleys of our state first began to be colonized. They are interesting because they are peculiar, not because they have had a very great effect upon the population of the state. The first is the coming of the Mormons into the country. These religious people, with their strange beliefs and practices, were compelled to leave their homes in Illinois in 1844. The next year they took up their journey westward and crossed the Missouri at two or three places. The main colony gathered about six miles north of the present site of Omaha, where their town was called "Winter Quarters." In two years the settlement grew to 15,000 inhabitants. Such things as the country offered, they took for food and shelter. The amount of forage and timber required to sustain such a fair sized city was not small, and the removal of forests and game disturbed the Indians. The land belonged to the Red Man, and the government was compelled to stand by his rights. The Mormons had to move. From this place they scattered, some crossing the Missouri and others making the long, tedious journey to a new home at Salt Lake. Settlements were made here and there by Mormon families, and in some places enough of them collected to maintain

THE MOR- MONS.

3

a church.   As late as 1857 they made a settlement at Genoa, now in the eastern part of Nance
County.   A hundred families received shares of
GENOA. the thousand acres which they inclosed
and in a few years their colony was very
prosperous.   But the Indians again interfered,
for the Pawnees came to occupy the reservation
assigned them by the government.   Wars between the Pawnees and the Sioux constantly annoyed them, and in five or six years after Genoa
was founded, the Mormons had again dispersed to
other parts.   At that place are left only earth-
works to mark their former abode.

The second feature of interest is the wonderful
gold panic which seized the people of the East,
when it was announced in 1849 that gold had
been discovered in California.   The valley of the
Platte was the natural avenue by which to approach the mountains, especially from the northern states.   People arrived in great numbers
THE GOLD HUNT-ERS. at the places where the Missouri was
crossed, and for a short time the fords of
the river were crowded.   They made their
way across the plains with such means as they
had, either on foot, or with the ox-team, or on
horse-back.   Ill prepared for the most part, many
perished in the long marches.   A few gave up
their hope of finding riches and began life as
pioneers in the new country.   They were among
the early settlers of Nebraska, but their number
was not large.   One must have a strong imagina-

tion to realize even dimly the long lines of toilers across the continent, the hardships and the heart-aches, and the terrible suffering, which left the whole way marked by castaway garments, by beasts of burden that had perished, and by graves of weary pilgrims. This sad picture points to a moral about fortune-hunting.[1]

---

[1] Johnson, *History of Nebraska*, 98–100. Schouler, *History of U. S.*, V., 130–148.

V.—THE ACQUISITION OF THE
TERRITORY.

Before the organization of the country into
territories can be discussed, it is necessary to
know how the United States came to own it.
When the thirteen original states banded themselves together into a nation in 1788, the people
and their representatives in Congress did not look
beyond the Mississippi River. This was the western boundary as mentioned in the treaty of 1783
THE between the United States and Great Brit-
MIS- ain. Spain held the land west of this
SOURI
AS A river, which long before had been named
BOUND-
ARY. Louisiana for Louis XIV. When two nations hold opposite banks of a stream, it is understood that both have a right to use it, each one owning to the center. In the case of this river, not only
did Spain possess the land on the west, but the
mouth was entirely in Spanish territory. There
Spain owned both sides. All went well as long as
the commerce of the people living west of the Al-
leghenies was allowed to pass into the Gulf. But
Spain was not to be depended on and sometimes
closed the mouth of the river. This caused bad
feeling between the two nations concerned, and
made it very desirable for the United States to
obtain at least all of the east bank of the river, if
opportunity offered itself. In one of the turns of

European politics in 1800, Spain gave to France the whole country west of the Mississippi, as far as Spanish claims extended. Thomas Jefferson, just elected president, saw a chance for the United States to buy a portion from France. He therefore told Mr. Livingstone, minister at Paris, to try to make the purchase, and in May, 1803, Monroe also was sent to France to aid him. At **THE PURCHASE.** length Napoleon decided to cede the whole of Louisiana to the United States. This seems to have come about, not through the skill of the men trying to make the purchase, but because of the condition in which the affairs of France were at that time. The price of this whole country, from the Mississippi to the Rocky Mountains, and from the Gulf of Mexico to British America, was $15,000,000. In the treaty there is nothing said about boundaries. To the northwest very little was known accurately about the extent of the claim, so that little could be said.

A moment's thought makes plain how great a difference this purchase has made in the growth of the United States. What would the career of the Union have been, hemmed in by the Mississippi, with European nations on the west? What **EFFECT UPON THE NATION.** great success this change has brought to the idea of a Republic! How much more dignity and importance among the nations of the world this growth to a land empire has given to the United States! Together with other additions to our domain, it has made the

Nation more symmetrical, and has thrown under one flag the slopes of the great Mississippi and Missouri valleys. Who will say that by the acquisition of this 900,000 square miles of territory the controlling influence in North America, and perhaps in the Western Hemisphere, did not pass to the United States?

Very soon after the purchase Congress took steps to form the country into one or more territories, and to extend the laws formally over the land. From that time the maps showed various divisions, but until the prairies were peopled the changes were of small importance. It was mostly "*Indian Country*" until 1854.

AUTHORITIES AND BOOKS OF REFERENCE.

Henry Adams, *Hist. of U. S. during 1st Administration of Th. Jefferson*, II., Chaps. II.-VI.
Von Holst, *Hist. of U. S., 1750-1832*, Chap. V., pp. 183-188.
Schouler, *Hist. of U. S.*, II., 36-52.
Johnson, *Hist. of Nebraska*, 44-46, giving a text of the treaty.
Morse, *Thomas Jefferson*, 231.
The American Statesman, 203-210.

VI. — THE KANSAS–NEBRASKA ACT IN CONGRESS.[1]

The beginning of the history of Nebraska as a territory must be studied in the records of Congress. Long before there were white people enough in the valley of the Platte to make a small dinner party, the law-makers at Washington had **HISTORY OF THE TERRITORY BEGINS IN POLITICS.** begun to think about forming a territory. Government was not needed there yet. It was a political matter. The questions about the Oregon boundary, the settlements in California, the Republic of Texas, and the new territory acquired from Mexico constantly drew the attention of Congress to matters beyond the Mississippi River. The subject of a new territory at the mouth of the Platte River arose in 1844, ten years before a bill establishing it was really passed by Congress and signed by the president. Efforts were made several times between 1844 and 1854 to bring this about, and chief among the men interested in it

---

[1] This was called the *Nebraska and Kansas Bill*, or the *Nebraska Bill*, during the debates upon it in Congress. The name *Nebraska* was first suggested as a name for the Territory by William Wilkins, Secretary of War, in his annual report, on November 30, 1844. He wrote: "The Platt or Nebraska, being the central stream leading into or from the Great South Pass, would very properly furnish a name for the Territory, which I propose suggesting to be erected into a territorial government." *Congressional Globe*, 1st Sess., 33d Cong., App., p. 715.

was Stephen A. Douglas. He was a democrat, and a very shrewd politician. He began his career in Congress in 1843 as a representative from Illinois. In 1847 he entered the Senate, where he served for twelve years. Mr. Douglas was very prominent in the discussions which led to the organization of Nebraska, and a study of the bill by which this was done rightly begins with a study of him.

STE-
PHEN A.
DOUG-
LAS.

He was prime mover in urging the subject upon Congress. His motives, his ambition, his schemes, all are a part of the history of Nebraska. The influence of this man and the acts of Congress from 1844 to 1854 are not alone sufficient to show the reason why Nebraska became a territory when it did. The subject of slavery entered almost everything that was done in Congress for years before Nebraska was organized. Trouble arose in Congress whenever new territories were made, because slave-holders wanted slavery allowed and the opposers of slavery at the North desired to prohibit the whole evil. There had been an agreement in Congress in 1820, which readers of American History are familiar with under the name of the Missouri Compromise.

SLAV-
ERY
AND
THE
MISSOU-
RI COM-
PRO-
MISE.

By this bill anti-slavery men in Congress had consented not to interfere with the question of slavery in the Southwest. On the other hand, the slavery men had agreed not to introduce slavery into the Louisiana Purchase, north of the parallel of latitude 36° 30'. Although Missouri is north of that line, slavery was not prohibited within its limits. Mr. Douglas claimed that the *Compromise of 1850* took the place of the

THE COMPROMISE OF 1850. *Missouri Compromise*, because, as he said, the former allowed a territory to have slaves or not, just as it chose. This was not true, but it served as his pretext. He was the chairman of the Committee on Territories, and reported to the Senate on January 23, 1854, a bill which provided for two territories. In the previous bills only one was mentioned. Mr. Douglas was the author of the section of the bill

SQUATTER SOVEREIGNTY which contained the idea of a territory regulating slavery within its own boundaries. This doctrine is called "Popular Sovereignty" or "Squatter Sovereignty." From the time when the news of the bill spread through

EFFECT OF THE KANSAS-NEBRASKA BILL. **(a) On Congress** **(b) On the People.** the country, every community was stirred up over the subject. In Congress the greatest struggle in its history took place. "Why should this bill cause such a commotion?" may be asked. It re-opened the question of slavery, which many supposed to have been settled by the compromises. The Kansas-Nebraska Bill, as it is called, brought on the contest between the supporters and the opposers of slavery. It destroyed the Whig party, and divided the people on the subject of slavery alone. The new Republican Party, whose purpose at first was to prevent the spread of slavery

and afterwards to stop it altogether, dates from this
(c)On   time. Inhabitants of Nebraska probably
Parties. are not proud of the fact that the bill
which organized the valley of the Platte into a
territory came from those who upheld slavery,
and that it was passed by their votes.[1]   But they
may be glad that the schemes of Mr. Douglas
helped only to unite the parties of the North
against the one great curse of the Nation, and led
directly to the freedom of the slaves.   The idea
of Popular Sovereignty is not that splendid principle that *the will of a people shall rule supreme*,
but only a mockery of it.

AUTHORITIES AND BOOKS OF REFERENCE.

Von Holst, *History of U. S., 1850–1854.* Chaps. VI.–VIII.
Schouler, *History of the U. S.*, V., 276–292.
Congressional Globe,Vol. 28, pt. I., 33d Cong. 1st session, p.
221, etc.
Seward's Works (Boston, 1884), IV., 433–479.
Johnson, *Hist. Amer. Politics* (N. Y., 1884), 157–166.
Sterne, *Const. Hist. and Political Development of U. S.*, 186–
192.
Young, *American Statesman.* 940–960; Chaps. 75 and 76.
Shepard, *Martin Van Buren*, 376–379.
Roosevelt, *T. H. Benton*, 315–349.
Mag of Amer. Hist., XVIII., 478.
Spencer, *Hist. of U. S.*, III., 504–6.
Crafts, *Hist. of U. S. of Amer.*, I.,578–580.
Andrews, *Brief Institutes of our Const. Hist.*, 226.
Davis, *Rise and Fall of Confed. Gov't.*, I., Chap. V.
Lalor *Cyclopedia of Pol. Sci.*, II., 667–670.

SUGGESTIVE TOPICS AND QUESTIONS.

What was the Oregon Boundary matter? See Barrow's
Oregon (*Commonwealth Series*).
Schouler, *Hist. of U. S.*, IV., 504–514.
How did California come to be a part of the U. S.?   See

---

[1] In its final form, the Kansas-Nebraska bill passed the House May
22, 1854, by a vote of 113 to 100. The Senate approved it three days
later by a vote of 35 to 13, and the President signed it on May 30, 1854.

Schouler, *Hist. of U. S.*, IV., 247, 445–7, 528–535.

When did Texas become a republic and how long was it independent? See Schouler, V., index.

Was Douglas sincere in his views? Read speeches of Douglas and Lincoln.

VII.—THE BILL ITSELF.[1]

The law passed by Congress to organize the territory of Nebraska resembles an old law of the Continental Congress. Indeed, every time that Congress has passed a law to form a territory, the Ordinance of 1787, as this old law is called, has been the model for it. An act or law which organizes a territorial government, naming the boundaries, the officers, and the manner of their appointment, is called the *Organic Act.* Such for our territory was the part of the Kansas-Nebraska act which relates to Nebraska. The whole bill consists of thirty-seven sections, of which the first eighteen apply to Nebraska alone. Three departments were made, just as in the constitutions of the United States and of each state. The general plan is the same everywhere in this Republic, and the territorial constitution, as might have been expected, provided for governor, legislature, and supreme court. The first governor of a territory in the United States was appointed by the President and Senate, and this mode of appointment has not been changed. In the same manner, a secretary, attorney, and marshal received their offices. The secretary had a term of five years, but the others, including the

ORDI-
NANCE
OF
1787.

ORGAN-
IC ACT.

EXECU-
TIVE
OFFI-
CERS.

---

[1] *United States Statutes*, X., 277.

governor, had one of but four years. It is interesting to note that since the time of the *Ordinance of 1787* these terms of office had increased
by one year.

The fourth section of the bill provided for a
council of thirteen members and a house of twenty-
six. The governor had the usual veto upon legislation, which began in 1787 with absolute power
to forbid a bill to become a law. It was very soon
modified, however, so that a certain majority of
members could pass bills over his veto. The
three judges of the supreme court received their
appointment in the same manner as the governor.

**LEGIS-
LA-
TURE.** This territory had the very same kind of
representation in Congress as the old Northwest Territory had under the Ordinance of
1787, namely, a delegate to the House of Representatives, with right to discuss and advise concerning the territory, but without right to vote. One
**TERRI-
TORIAL
DELE-
GATE.** of the important provisions of the bill
(Sec. 16) reserved two square miles out of
each township for purposes of education,
but it seems that Nebraska received no benefit
from this while a territory.[1] There are certain
things in the Organic act that show in whose interest the bill was made and by whose votes it
was passed. (1) The voters are only the "white"
population (Sec. 5). (2) It is especially stated
that the two acts of Congress of the years 1793
and 1850, about fugitive slaves, should be in force

---

[1] Governor's Message, 9th Session.

in the territory (Secs. 9 and 10). (3) In the last
half of the 14th section, the Missouri Compromise
act is declared of no effect, and the idea of non-
intervention by Congress is expressed. This idea
was that Congress should not interfere with any
state in its own private affairs: that the people
should regulate their domestic institutions in their
own way, subject only to the Constitution of the
United States. This is the doctrine of "Popular
Sovereignty." At the time the old Ordinance
of 1787 was passed, there was little opposition
when Nathan Dane, a Massachusetts lawyer,
moved to add a paragraph prohibiting slavery
in the territory north of the Ohio River. Between that time and 1854 things had changed.
It was no longer possible to pass a bill with a
clause in it prohibiting slavery in a territory,
although the land might lie farther north than the
Ohio River. The Ordinance of 1787 was the
first act of the United States that contained a fugitive slave clause and the Kansas-Nebraska Bill
was the last.[1]

_____

[1]This latter statement remains to be verified, but seems to be true

VIII.—THE TERRITORY OF NEBRASKA.

When the territory of Oregon was established in 1848, the summit of the Rocky Mountains between the parallels of 42° and 49° became a part of the boundary. In 1850, at the formation of Utah Territory, the same mountains were made the eastern boundary between the 30th and 40th **BOUND-** parallels. When Nebraska was organ- **ARIES.** ized, the summit of the Rockies easily became the western limit, because it was already a boundary line. Just where the "summit of the Rocky Mountains" is, the members of Congress themselves probably did not know. In Map IV. it is taken as the water-shed, on one side of which the rivers flow to the Gulf of Mexico and on the other to the Pacific Ocean. The western boundary of Minnesota, which was formed into a territory five years before Nebraska, followed the Missouri towards the northwest as far as White Earth River, and then turned northward along this stream to the British line. The northeast boundary of the Territory of Nebraska likewise followed these rivers.[1]

No one need think that the exact location of these lines which Congress had fixed, except the boundary between Kansas and Nebraska, made

---

[1] White Earth River rises south of British America. Doubtless the boundary would be completed by a line drawn north from the source of this river to the 49th parallel.

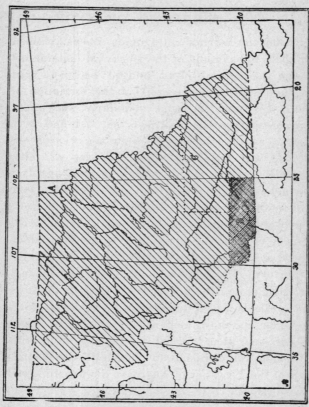

MAP IV. TERRITORY OF NEBRASKA, 1854-1861.

A. White Earth River.
B. Portion removed by formation of Colorado.
C. Present Limits.

any difference at all between the inhabitants of
the Territory. The few white persons in the
country were at the southeast corner, and the Red
Man knew no boundaries. Since the western
country was being settled rapidly, these extensive
limits could not long remain. In February, 1861,
Colorado Territory was created, taking a small
piece out of the southwestern corner of Nebraska.
Two months later Dakota Territory was formed,
which removed all the stretch of country north of
the 43d parallel. At the same time two tracts
were added to Nebraska from Utah and Washington territories. The effect was to change the
western boundary from the indefinite "summit of
the Rocky Mountains" to the 33d meridian west
of Washington. Nebraska Territory was now
nearly four times as long as it was wide, stretching in fact, about fifteen degrees in longitude.

It so remained for two years. At the formation
of Idaho Territory, March, 1863, all west of the
27th meridian was taken away. With these def-
inite boundaries it remained, even after it became
a state in 1867.

The organization of the Territory of Nebraska
begins with the appointment of Francis Burt, of
South Carolina, as governor, by the president,
Franklin Pierce. With the arrival of Mr.
**ORGAN-
IZA-
TION.** Burt at Bellevue, October 7, 1854, came
the enforcement of law in the new settle-
ments. Hardly had the governor begun his work
when he died, and the secretary, T. B. Cuming,

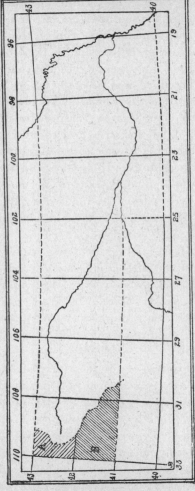

MAP V. TERRITORY OF NEBRASKA FROM 1861 TO 1863.

A.   Part added from Washington Territory.

B.   Part added from Utah Territory.

became acting governor, as the bill provided. By
the hand of the latter the wheels of government were set in motion. First, districts were
laid out in order that a census might be taken.
After the population had been ascertained, the
FIRST STEPS. thirteen councilmen and twenty-six representatives were apportioned for election
among eight districts or counties.[1] On election day, December 12, not only were members
of the legislature selected, but also a delegate for
Congress. The returns showed a voting population of 800, but some allowance must be made for
the tendency of non-residents to come across the
river to vote. The acting governor assigned the
three judges to districts, set the time for holding
terms of court, and appointed county officers.
Members of the legislature were duly elected, and
the government of the Territory had started.

The history of the legislature of the Territory

---

[1]The following shows the first eight counties, with the vote of each
for delegate to Congress, and the number of councilmen and representatives assigned:—

NORTH PLATTE				SOUTH PLATTE			
COUNTY	VOTE	No. Coun.	No. Rep.	COUNTY	VOTE	No. Coun.	No. Rep.
Douglas	297	4	8	Cass	130	1	2
Burt	57	1	2	Pierce	188	3	5
Dodge	14	1	2	Fortney	42	1	2
Washington	34	1	2	Richardson	38	1	2
	402	7	14		398	6	9

There was from the start a struggle for the capital between the various places, especially between the regions north and south of the Platte.
These figures are of use in the study of that subject.

consists of twelve regular sessions, of which the
first began January 16, 1855, and the last one
January 10, 1867. The time of meeting was
often changed, however. The second session began in December, the third in January,
LEGISLA-
TION. and the fourth in December. From the
fourth to the eighth sessions inclusive, the opening day fell in the latter part of the year, while
for the four remaining it was changed back to
January. From 1855 to 1867 twelve yearly sessions were held, with the exception of the year
1863.[1] The membership of the house of represen-
tatives was increased from twenty-six to
MEM-
BER-
SHIP OF thirty-five at the second session, and later
LEGIS-
LA- to thirty-nine, the limit set by the Kan-
TURE. sas-Nebraska Bill. There was no change
in the number of members in the council.

Law-making in a territory is different in many
respects from the same thing in a state. In the
latter, the power of the body that makes the law
is very much restricted by the constitution. In
almost every state in the Union there is a long
list of subjects concerning which the legislature
is forbidden to make special laws. It is
GENER-
AL AND thought better to make general laws that
SPE-
CIAL apply to all the cases of the same kind.
LAWS. For example, the legislature of Nebraska
is forbidden to make a charter for any particular
city. But a law may be made applying to all the

---

[1] This was in the middle of the war, when money was scarce. The
financial reason is the only one assigned for the failure to hold a session
in that year.

cities of a certain class, the class being determined by population. But the territorial legislature was not restricted at all in this regard, and laws upon all sorts of special subjects are found in the statutes. Divorces were granted by act of the legislature, every town was formed by a separate law, and the territorial assembly smiled upon every academy and "university," which lived, perhaps, only upon paper. But the Territory of Nebraska did not continue through the whole period to make law in so clumsy a manner. Gradually the work of legislation was made more expeditious by the passage of general acts on various subjects. A law of 1864 gave the courts jurisdiction of the subject of divorce. Another law was passed by which companies could be organized by taking certain legal steps, instead of asking the legislature to attend to every individual case. By one of the acts at the first session, a great part of the statutes of Iowa became the laws of the Territory. This is a good illustration of how a newly organized community gets its laws. At first all the states had a common model to follow in the English Statutes, which had accumulated for many centuries. But as soon as one state had excellent laws, it was an easy matter for another state to adopt them. This adoption of statutes has prevailed to a large extent in the western states, where the laws of New York, Pennsylvania, Ohio, and Michigan have repeatedly been copied. Part of the Iowa laws

[margin note:] DEVELOPMENT TO GENERAL LAWS.

thus brought into Nebraska defines crimes and
their punishment, and part of them regulates civil
processes, such as the manner of bringing suits,
etc.   The former is called a *criminal code* and
the latter a *code of civil procedure.*   The territorial legislature at its third session foolishly repealed both these and left no others in place of

REPEAL OF THE LAWS. them.   Governor Cuming told the fourth
legislature that the laws were "limited,
confused, and contradictory," and that
careful legislation was necessary.   The question
of the removal of the capitol was uppermost in
the minds of the representatives, and adjournment
came without the needed laws.   In the autumn of
1858, Govenor Richardson called the legislature
in special session, three months before the regular time, principally to pass laws in place of those

ACTS OF THE FIFTH SESSION. that had been repealed.   Many of the
criminal laws enacted at this fifth, or spe-
cial session, remained in force until 1873,
when the criminal code of Ohio was
adopted.   At the same time civil laws also were
passed, which were re-enacted in 1866.

The earliest liquor law of Nebraska was the
most stringent.   The first legislature in 1855 prohibited not only the manufacture of liquor in the

AN EARLY LIQUOR LAW. Territory, but also selling, exchanging,
and giving intoxicating drinks.   In 1858
this was modified by a license law.   Slavery in Nebraska and Kansas is of special interest.   In Kansas was fought the real battle of the

frontier, between the slavery and anti-slavery factions, and one can appreciate the victory only by reading the history of that time. Nebraska Territory knew little of the conflict because slave labor **SLAV-** was unprofitable so far north. Yet there **ERY.** were some slaves even in the small settlements here, for the territorial officers who came from the Southern States brought slaves with them. Opinions on both sides of the question are found in the Journals of the legislature. There were attempts to make it unlawful for a free negro to settle in the Territory, and bills were introduced to prevent slavery altogether within the limits of Nebraska. The history of the Territory is closely connected with the subject of abolition, in the career of John Brown, who spent much time in the southeastern counties just be- **JOHN** fore the war, helping fugitive slaves to **BROWN.** escape from Kansas by his so-called "underground railway." This was a special route, of which Falls City was the first station in the Territory, and Nebraska City or Brownville the second, where runaway slaves crossed the river on their way to Canada. By this means many a negro sought and gained his freedom.

The Federal Government paid the salaries of the governor, secretary, judges, and members of the legislature, while the attorney-general and **FINANCES.** marshal received only fees. For this reason, the expenses of the territory were comparatively light. It seems that the lands re-

served for school purposes could not be used during the territorial period.[1] This threw the expense of establishing a school system upon the people, which with other matters of expenditure
DEBT. caused a small debt to accumulate. It is easiest for a city or state to raise money by issuing bonds bearing interest for a number of years. The territory did this, but the debt incurred was never large. Resources were usually larger than liabilities in the accounts of the treasurer and auditor. The laws of the Territory
REV-ENUE LAWS. concerning taxation were poor, so that money came into the treasury slowly. Governor Cuming spoke of the revenue laws in his message to the fourth legislature, as "inapplicable and almost inoperative." Of course the taxes increased with the growth of population. The financial reports show that all the money paid in 1856 came from three counties and amounted to $1,236.00. The annual revenues for ten years,
What Does a Territorial Government Cost? beginning with 1856, averaged over $10,-000.00. In 1865 the annual taxes had reached nearly $54,000.00. This may be said to be what it cost the people directly to carry on the territorial government. There are many other things, however, that should be added to this to find the real cost, such as the fees received by the attorney and marshal. There may also be added to the territorial expenses paid by the people the annual appropriation

---

[1] Governor's Message, 9th session.

by the Federal Government of about $17,000.00
for salaries, and large amounts for improvements.
Among the latter was an item of $50,000.00,
granted for a road between Omaha and Kearney.
When a movement was started to form a state
government, opponents argued that a territory
costs less than a state. In the case of a country
like Nebraska, into which the tide of population
was fairly rushing, the expenses of the territory
and of the state which follows are not to be
compared.

Life in the Territory of Nebraska was not without its exciting political quarrels. The most
bitter fights in politics are over the location of
county seats and state capitals, and this was sadly
true here. The death of Governor Burt, who in-
THE CAPI-TAL FIGHT. tended to make Bellevue the capital, gave
the acting governor an opportunity to de-
cide upon Omaha instead. Intense feeling was aroused at once. From this time on the
Territory never lacked sites for the capitol. The
pull was both north and south, to Florence, Platts-
mouth, Nebraska City, and the interior of the
country. In 1855, 1857, 1858, and 1867, the
strife between the North and South Platte regions
was mentioned with regret by the governors
in their messages to the legislature. One governor argued that a bridge across the Platte
would tend to allay the feeling. At the fourth
session, part of the legislature actually withdrew
to Florence, north of Omaha, but the move was

unsuccessful.   A bill had been introduced into
the previous legislature, 1857, concerning a removal of the capital from Omaha to a town by the
name of Douglas, Lancaster County, which existed only on paper.   A writer who took part in
the politics of that time says that the apportionment of members for the first legislature was
made in such a way that the members would sustain Governor Cuming's decision, when the question of the location of the capital came before
them.[1]

The wonderful settlement of the western country is naturally a subject of inquiry.   What led
people westward in such numbers?   The discovery
of gold in California late in the forties first in-
duced people to turn their faces toward the Pacific.   Five or six years after this, the Kansas-
Nebraska bill by its prominence advertised the
Great Plains, and in 1859 gold was discovered at
Pike's Peak.   The effect of this discovery,
CAUSES, RAPIDI-TY, AND EXTENT OF SET-TLE-MENTS. coming during hard times, was probably
much greater than it otherwise would have
been.   The exceptional advantages offered
to all classes by a new country accounts
largely for the tide of immigration. The pre-emp-
tion and homestead laws of the United States
served to bring the matter of lands and homes
more sharply to the attention of eastern citizens

---

1 J. S. Morton, in *State Hist. Soc. Pub.*, III., 103.   A comparison of
each apportionment and the political majorities of the counties in each
district afford room for special study. See Fiske, *Civil Government*, 216.

and promised them undisputed possession of western farms. The rapid settlement of Nebraska, too, was made, notwithstanding the unfavorable opinion in the East about the quality of Nebraska soil. Had the toiling farmer of New York and Ohio known that in a few years Nebraska would outrank all the other states in its yield of corn per acre, would not the rate of immigration have been more surprising? The settlements, as a rule, proceeded from the Missouri River westward. Some particular circumstance here and there, such as the location of a fort, led settlers to go far out on the frontier to make homes for themselves. There was also a tendency to settle near the usually traveled wagon routes, along which freighters stopped on their way to Pike's Peak, Utah, and California. In 1859 the white population extended from the river 140 miles westward, and the number of counties had grown from eight in 1855 to thirty-five four years later.

In this first decade great strides had been made towards accumulating material wealth and establishing prosperous homes. Population had increased marvelously. Assessors' rolls for the year **WEALTH OF THE TERRITORY.** 1866 showed a million and a half of dollars invested in merchandise, $143,000.00 in manufactures, and upwards of $85,-000.00 in household furniture. For that time such material progress means much. Agriculture was firmly established, and the richness of the soil of Nebraska was abundantly proved. The value of farm stock lacked little of three million dollars. Altogether the wealth of the Territory was placed at eighteen millions.

IX.—THE STATE.

Before the Territory was scarcely five years
old, the question of changing to a state government began to be discussed. The greater part of
the message of Governor Black to the leg-
**FORMA-
TION.** islature in December, 1859, was devoted
to it,[1] and that body passed a bill providing for an election in March, 1860, to decide
whether or not a state organization should be
effected.[2] The vote of the people favored the con-
tinuance of the territorial form. The
**FIRST
AT-
TEMPT.** subject appears not to have been discussed seriously for four years. In February, 1864, the legislature asked Congress to
permit Nebraska to become a state,[3] and about
two months later their petition was granted in the
passage of an *"Enabling Act."* However
**ENA-
BLING
ACT.** the only action taken in Nebraska under
this provision was to elect members to a
convention, which met and adjourned without ac-
complishing its purpose. The legislature did
not discuss the subject again until the session of
1866. This time it was left to no "constitutional
convention" to draw up a constitution, but that
work was done by a committee and was submitted

1 *Council Journal*, 6th Sess., 15–22.
2 *Laws of Territory*, 1860, pp., 45–48. Johnson, *Hist. of Neb.*, 120.
3 *Laws of Territory*, 1864, pp., 282, 283.

to the people for approval on June 2.[1] The contest was very close and exciting, and the new form of government was adopted by a majority **CONSTI-** of only one hundred out of nearly 7,800 **TUTION** **OF 1866.** votes cast.[2] Two political parties, taking opposites of the question, nominated full sets of officers and completed a thorough organization. The republicans favored and the democrats opposed the adoption of the new constitution. In their stump speeches the orators talked only about the advisability of state government or no state government, but the political leaders were mainly concerned with the effect of the issue upon national politics.

From the election in June until early in 1867, Nebraska had both a territorial and a state form of government. The authorities of the **TWO** Territory continued in office, and the ter- **LEGIS-** **LA-** ritorial legislature, on January 10, 1867, **TURES** **AT** met for its twelfth and last session. Mean- **ONCE.** while, the new state legislature had its first meeting July 4, 1866, and was again called together February 20, 1867, only two days after the last territorial legislature had adjourned, in order to accept a certain requirement imposed by the Federal Government.

The constitution of 1866 was not satisfactory to a large number of people, so that a convention to draw up another was authorized by the

---

1 *Council Journal,* 11th Sess., 129, 170, 184.
2 Johnson, *Hist. of Neb.,* 128. Vote: 3938 to 3838.

legislature at its eighth session.[1] The election of
NEW CON- members of the convention came in May.
STITU- The document which they drew up was
TIONS. submitted to the people for their approval,
September 19, 1871. Several amendments were
ONE proposed, each of which aroused the oppo-
PRO-
POSED sition of a particular class. One pro-
IN 1871. vided for the taxation of church property,
another for compulsory education, and a third
that counties and cities should not vote aid to cor-
porations, such as railroads. Five such amendments were voted on separately, and all were rejected along with the constitution itself.[2] Four
ONE years later, on October 12, 1875, the peo-
ADOPT-
ED IN ple adopted a more satisfactory constitu-
1875. tion.[3] At the same time two separate
propositions voted upon were also approved. The
constitution of 1875 went into effect November 1,
of that year, and still continues almost unchanged
(1892).

From 1866 to 1891 inclusive, twenty-two sessions of the state legislature have been held.[4]

---

1 *Statutes*, 1871, 63–66.

2 Vote: for, 7986; against, 8627. Johnson, *Hist. of Neb.*, 145.

3 Vote: for, 30202; against, 5474. Johnson, *Hist. of Neb.*, 151.

4 The following are the twenty-two sessions. Those marked * were
special or extra sessions:

1.	July 4–11, 1866.	11.	January 7–Feb. 25, 1875.
*2.	Feb. 20–21, 1·67.	*12.	Dec. 5, 1876.
3.	May 16–June 24. 1867.	*13.	Dec. 5, 1876.
*4.	Oct. 27–28, 1868.	14.	Jan. 2–Feb. 15, 1877.
5.	Jan. 7–Feb. 15, 1869.	15.	Jan 7–Feb. 25. 1879.
*6.	Feb. 17–March 4, 1870.	16.	Jan. 4–Feb. 26, 1881: 40 days.
*7.	March 4. 1870.	*17.	May 10–24, 1882.
8.	Jan. 5–Mar. 28; May 30–June	18.	Jan. 2–Feb. 26, 1883: 42 days.
	6, 1871.	19.	Jan. 6–Mar. 5, 1885: 43 days.
	8th Adjourned. Jan. 9–19, 1872.	20.	Jan. 4–Mar. 31, 1887: 61 days.
9.	January 9–Mar. 3, 1873.	21.	Jan. 1–Mar. 30, 1889: 67 days.
*10.	Mar. 27–29, 1873.	22.	Jan. 6–April 4, 1891: 71 days.

The first constitution allowed biennial sessions of **LEGISLA-** forty days each, which was not changed **TURE.** by the constitution of 1875. There were several special or "called" sessions, and one "adjourned" session, which varied somewhat in length.

Nine meetings were very short.[1] The **SHORT** seventh met but one day, and the twelfth **SES-** **SIONS.** and thirteenth were both held on the fifth of December, 1876.[2] As the state grew in population and wealth, its interests largely increased and the legislature found it difficult to transact all the necessary business in the allotted forty days. This length of time was exceeded by two **CHANGE** days at the eighteenth session, and by **IN NUM-** **BER OF** three days at the nineteenth session. At **DAYS.** the latter meeting, in 1885, an amendment to the constitution was proposed by the legislature, making sixty days the length of a session instead of forty. At the election of 1886, this was voted upon and carried.[3] The last three legislatures sat for sixty-one, sixty-seven, and seventy-one days respectively.

Under the first constitution the number of senators was fixed for ten years at thirteen, and the

---

[1] These were 1st, 2d, 4th, 7th, 8th Adjourned, 10th, 12th, 13th, 17th.

[2] The governor brought the legislature together on the morning of that day to canvass the votes for presidential electors. This was accomplished, the result showing the election of Amasa Cobb, A. H. Conner, and S. A. Strickland. A question had arisen concerning the eligibility of Mr. Cobb to be an elector, and the governor convened the legislature again at 3 P.M. of the same day, to settle this matter and to canvass the votes for state officers. This was all the business done at the twelfth and thirteenth sessions. *Senate Journal,* 12-14 Sess., 1-33.

[3] *Session Laws,* 1885, p. 435. *House Journal,* 1887, pp. 969-972.

number of representatives at thirty-nine, the
MEM-BER-SHIP. limits of membership being twenty-five and seventy-five. By the constitution of 1875 these limits were increased to thirty-three and one hundred. The full numbers are now elected.

The seven governors that have been elected in the State have each served two terms, on the average.[1] Since 1867 the duties of governor have seldom devolved upon acting governors, while in **GOVERN-ORS.** the Territory the acting governor was often in office. Under the constitution of 1866 the secretary performed the duties belonging to the head of the State, if the latter died or was removed. This happened in 1871, when Governor Butler was impeached. W. H. James took his place, remaining in office until the term of the next governor began, in 1873.

During the territorial period and also the early years of state history, there were three **JUDI-CIARY.** judicial districts. In 1883 the number had increased to ten, and in 1891 to fifteen. The supreme court has remained, from the beginning of the Territory in 1854, a body of three members.[2] The two senators al-

---

[1] The list is as follows:

1.—David Butler, Feb. 21, 1867.   4.—Albinus Nance, Jan. 9, 1879.
2.—Rob't W. Furnas, Jan. 13, 1873.   5.—James W. Dawes, Jan. 4, 1883.
3.—Silas Garber, Jan. 11, 1875.   6.—John M. Thayer, Jan. 9, 1887.
          7.—James E. Boyd, Jan. 8, 1891.

[2] The chief justices of the State have been as follows:

1.—W. A. Little, 1866.   6.—Amasa Cobb, Jan. 1, 1884.
2.—O. P. Mason, 1866.   7.—Samuel Maxwell, Jan 1, 1886.
3.—G. B. Lake, Jan. 16, 1873.   8.—M. B. Reese, Jan. 1, 1888.
4.—Daniel Gantt, Jan. 3, 1878.   9.—Amasa Cobb, Jan. 1, 1890.
5.—G. B. Lake, Jan. 1, 1882.   10.—Samuel Maxwell, Jan. 1, 1892.

5

lowed by the constitution of the United States
MEMBERS have represented Nebraska in Congress
OF CON- from the time of its admission,[1] but the
GRESS. number of congressmen has increased
from one in 1867, to six in 1893.[2]

Only the few who handle the money of a great
state or keep its accounts, know how much government costs and whence the money
FINANCES comes. Consideration of the system of
taxation is better left to the pages of civil government, but it is quite fitting to inquire at this
place how much money, in fact, is annually used
by the State. The cost of a territorial government was seen[3] to be very small, because it is
more simple, and also because part of the expense
falls upon the Federal Government. The num-

---

[1] The list of senators is as follows:

John M. Thayer, 1867–71.	Alvin Saunders, 1877–83.
Thomas W. Tipton, 1867–75.	C. H. Van Wyck, 1881–87.
Phineas W. Hitchcock, 1871–77.	Charles F. Manderson, 1883–1889.
Algernon S. Paddock, 1875–81.	Algernon S. Paddock, 1887–93;
	Charles F. Manderson, 1889–95.

[2] The congressmen have been as follows:

XXXIX. Congress............T. M. Marquett, (1867.)
XL.–XLII. Congress..........John Taffe, (1867–73.)
XLIII–XLIV. Congress....Lorenzo Crounse, (1873–77.)
XLV. Congress.................. { Frank Welsh, } (1877–79.) { T. J. Majors, }
XLVI.–XLVII. Congress...E. K. Valentine, (1879–83.)

XLVIII. Congress............ { 1st Dist.—A. J. Weaver............ } (1883–85.) { 2d Dist.—James Laird .... } { 3d Dist.—E. K. Valentine....... }

XLIX. Congress................ { 1st Dist.—A. J. Weaver............ } (1885–87.) { 2d Dist.—James Laird............. } { 3d Dist.—W. E. Dorsey .... }

L. Congress...................... { 1st Dist.—James A. McShane.. } (1887–89.) { 2d Dist.—James Laird............. } { 3d Dist.—Geo. W. E. Dorsey ... }

LI. Congress...................... { 1st Dist.—W. J. Connell.......... } (1889–91.) { 2d Dist.—G. L. Laws.............. } { 3d Dist.—Geo. W. E. Dorsey ... }

LII. Congress.................... { 1st Dist.—W. J. Bryan............. } (1891–93.) { 2d Dist.—W. A. McKeighan...... } { 3d Dist.—O. M. Kem .... }

[3] Above, p. 56.

ber both of people and officers is small. All the
life of the territory is on a less extensive scale.
As a state grows in population, the privations of
frontier life give way to a greater prosperity, at-
tended with luxuries. First, then, what does a
state government cost? The auditor makes his
reports every two years, and it is most
COST OF convenient to divide the time from 1869
A STATE
GOV- to 1890 into eleven periods of two years
ERN-
MENT. each. For one of these, on the average,
over two million dollars has been paid out, an
annual expense of one million dollars. In the
two years 1869 and 1870 the cost was $997,600.00.
In the years 1889 and 1890 it had increased to
$3,848,000.00. But this expense does not fall
more heavily upon the citizens of the State, than
did the small expense of the Territory upon its
citizens, because there are more to share it.

The funds of the state come partly from direct
taxes collected in each county and paid into the
SOUR- state treasury, and partly from lands
CES OF
REV- which have been reserved for a particular
ENUE.
purpose, as for education.

The old question about the location of the cap-
ital again arose at the final session of the terri-
torial legislature, but was not settled. At the
POLITI- fourth session of the state legislature, in
CAL May, 1867, the matters of apportionment
EVENTS. and removal of the capital had to be de-
cided, because they were included in the call of
Governor Butler for the special session. Even

as early as 1856 the census showed a greater
population south of the Platte than north of it,[1]
and the sectional struggle for proper representation finally resulted in a bill of the fourth legis-
LOCA-   lature, by which the seat of government
TION OF was to be removed to a place in either
CAPI-
TAL.   Seward, Saunders, Butler, or Lancaster
County. The governor, the secretary of state and
the auditor, by whom the site was to be selected,
chose its present location in Lancaster County,
where a city was immediately commenced. The
bill named this place *Lincoln*, in curious contrast
to the name *Douglas*, which had been proposed
by a territorial bill ten years before, when the
popularity of Stephen A. Douglas was at its
height.[2] Of great importance in the political
history of the State was the impeachment and
trial of the first governor. The process of such a
IM-   trial is better discussed in the chapters on
PEACH-
MENT civil government, and the exact truth of
OF GOV-
ERNOR. the matter can only be ascertained by a
careful study of the papers, diaries, letters, etc.,
of that time. Besides, in the case of a period so
recent as even the first years of the history of
this State, all matters of politics are best treated
merely as facts, without inquiry into motives.[3]

---

1 Cf. above, p. 51.

2 *State Hist. Soc. Pub.*, II., 66.

3 *House Journal*, 1871, pp. 392, 424, etc. *Impeachment Trial of David Butler*, Omaha, 1871. The impeachment resolutions were offered in the House on Feb. 28, 1871, and the trial by the Senate, sitting as a court, began March 14. The governor was removed from his office, although not found guilty of more than one of the charges.

The turbulent times of 1872, when the acting governor and the legislature were quarreling, were only steps in the departure of the State from disorder to system and law. The business of the public welfare soon became a more serious matter, and the acts of individual men became insignificant, compared with the interests of a great commonwealth. Few events of special **OTHER POLITICAL EVENTS** political importance have happened since that time. In 1876 the people of all parts of the Nation awaited anxiously the result of a petition concerning one of the electoral votes of Nebraska, because the presidential contest between Hayes and Tilden was very close. This matter, as well as the subject of citizenship involved in the Boyd-Thayer case of recent times, belongs to civil government.

X.—DEVELOPMENT OF THE RESOURCES OF NEBRASKA.

The great increase in the population of Nebraska is not surprising, in view of the richness **POPULA-** of the soil and the large demand every-**TION.** where for good agricultural lands. In 1880 little more than 450,000 people were found here, while in 1890 the census showed over a million.[1] Accurate statistics concerning the growth of a state or nation are very useful and instructive, because they show what parts of the population are increasing most rapidly. The growth in the past reveals something of the future. For example, the city population of the United States now increases much more rapidly than that of the country districts. In **GROWTH OF CITIES.** 1890 there were in this State sixteen cities of more than 2,500 inhabitants. Their total population was 290,000, or about two-fifths as many as lived in the country. Ten years earlier these same sixteen cities contained only about one-fifth as many. This opens the question of the cause of so much removal from the

---

[1] For statistics concerning population, see *Report of Sec., of State, Senate Journal*, 12th–14th Sess., 879–80; *State Agricultural Report, 1891*, p. 76. The following are given:—

1855	4494	1874	225257	1878	313748
1856	10716	1875	246280	1879	386410
1860	28841	1876	257747	1880	452542
1870	122993	1877	271561	1890	1058916

country to the city.[1] Nearly three hundred smaller cities and villages are scattered over the State, the

VIL-LAGES. highest number in any county being nine.[2] Nebraska stands twenty-sixth among the states of the Union in population. It has even less people to the square mile than the nation taken as a whole.[3] Density of population, how-

RANK AMONG STATES. ever, is not desirable for many reasons, not the least among which is the fact that the problems of government grow more difficult as the population increases.

Farming, stock-raising and manufactures have kept pace with the rapid development of population. The adaptation of the soil to corn-raising

AGRICUL-TURE. was well known to the Indians, and corn became the main crop as soon as farmers from the east began to turn the sod of their Nebraska homesteads.[4] In 1865, 53,000 acres were planted with corn, and 9,000 with wheat. The

CORN AND WHEAT. relative amounts of corn and wheat have varied much in the quarter of a century since that time, but on the whole much more land has been devoted to the former. For two seasons, 1871 and 1873, the amount of wheat was greater. Indeed, in the second of those years, the excess of wheat land was 31,000 acres. Since

---

[1] John Fiske, *Civil Govt., of the U. S.*, 119–120.

[2] Saunders and Richardson counties have nine each.

[3] People to the square mile: Nebraska, 13.8; Minnesota, 16.4; United States, 17.94; Texas, 8.5; Rhode Island, 318.2; Nevada, 0.4.

[4] The earliest homestead law of the United States was passed in 1862. A Nebraska pioneer by the name of Daniel Freeman secured the first homestead under this act. The place is about four miles west o Beatrice. Johnson, *Hist. of Neb.*, 896.

then, however, corn has been more in favor, the
the ratio in 1891 being 45 to 12.[1] Stock-raising
and manufactures in Nebraska are intimately connected with farming. The growing industry of
RELA- making beet sugar depends wholly upon
TION
OF farming, a large part of the stock-raisers
INDUS-
TRIES. are farmers who feed their own grain, and
packing houses look to the stockmen for their raw
material. Nebraska is not a mining region at all,
so that large industries that have gained a foot-
hold here, such as the smelting works in Omaha,
get their ore from beyond the limits of the State.
It is said that in the case of Colorado, never known
to the American people except as a gold state, the
value of farm products exceeds the value of ores
that are mined. Happily little wealth in Nebraska
is spent in mining, and the whole effort of the pro-
ducer is put into agriculture. Nebraska does not
compare favorably with other states in manufactures, because it has been settled so recently. In
agriculture, however, the State has a good record.
A comparatively small part of the land is now

[1]The following shows the number of acres of corn and wheat in
the State:

YEAR	ACRES		YEAR	ACRES		YEAR	ACRES	
	CORN	WHEAT		CORN	WHEAT		CORN	WHEAT
1865	53636	9241	1874	350000	311983	1883	2813303	1772990
1866	71503	9917	1875	700000	246938	1884	3235298	1950280
1867	64583	33333	1876	850000	376521	1885	3526475	1755252
1868	139082	36451	1877	1013158	376000	1886	3879123	1579727
1869	159952	56179	1878	1291000	1050000	1887	3865158	1642127
1870	172675	128333	1879	1522400	1154300	1888	4097067	1560021
1771	174168	177572	1880	1919600	1520315	1889	4097067	1404019
1872	200767	209836	1881	2149200	1958500	1890	4317682	1026821
1873	200000	231226	1882	2364120	1657000	1891	4538009	1223787

under cultivation, yet in the crops of 1890, Nebraska ranked ninth in corn, tenth in oats and twelfth in wheat. Who does not predict that when nearly all the available land of the State shall be tilled, here will be found the greatest yield to the acre and the largest harvests of farm products? Already Nebraska has ranked first in the yield of corn per acre.

With such generous returns from the soil, the people of the State have not been slow to spend large sums upon schools. Among the forty-four states, Nebraska stood only thirteenth in the amount of money spent upon education in 1889–90. Since admission into the Union a complete system of schools has been built up, **EDUCA-** which affords free instruction, from the **/TION.** primary grades even to special graduate work in the University. Not only were two sections of land out of each township set apart for the maintenance of the common schools, but the University and Normal School are also similarly endowed. The enterprise that called forth numerous "colleges" and "universities" before the territory was over two years old, has finally resulted in a splendid plan of education.

PART II.
Civil Government of Nebraska.

CIVIL
GOVERNMENT OF NEBRASKA.

I.—UNITED STATES LAND SURVEY.

The study of the origin of such divisions as states and territories belongs to civil government of the United States. The growth of civil institutions, the long development from the family to the state, cannot here be traced. The subject of civil government in Nebraska treats only of the peculiarities of this State, and may properly begin with the Federal land surveys within our borders.

Mr. Fiske has shown[1] the various divisions of land for purposes of government, both in the eastern and in the western states. It is the latter that especially concerns Nebraska. In the colonies no order was followed in county lines or in the limits of smaller districts. But an excellent system of boundaries has been adopted for all

BEGIN-NING OF U. S. LAND SUR-VEYS, 1785. the unsettled territory since acquired by the nation. By a law of the old Continental Congress in 1785, a plan of surveys was begun which used meridians and parallels as standards. The "*first principal me-*

[1] John Fiske, *Civil Government of the U. S.*, 71–88.

ridian" was drawn through the mouth of the Great Kenawha River, and afterwards became the western boundary of Ohio. As the public surveys were made further and further west, new meridians were established at intervals across the country, until the twenty-fourth was located near the Pacific coast. The "sixth principal meridian" is

SIXTH PRINCIPAL MERIDIAN. the one which concerns Nebraska. It runs through this State and Kansas, forming in Nebraska the western boundary of Jefferson, Saline, Seward, Butler, Stanton, and Wayne counties. On either side of it are *guide meridi-*

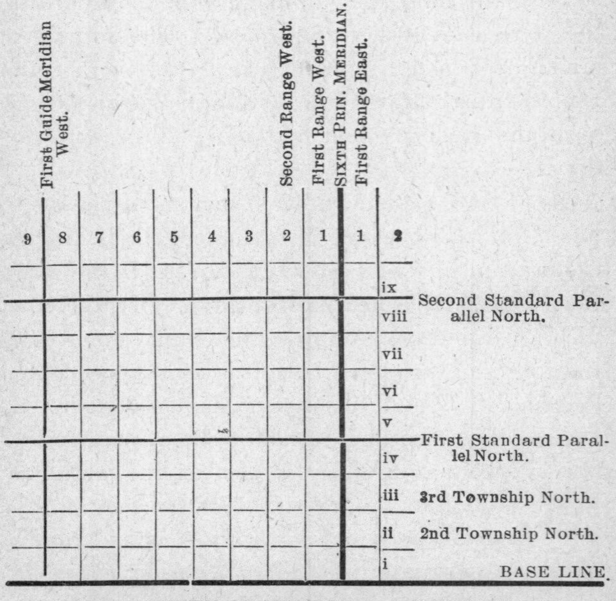

FIG. 1. SYSTEM OF MERIDIANS AND PARALLELS.

ans, forty-eight miles apart, one east and seven
west within the State. This interval of forty-eight
miles is further divided by seven intervening meridians, and the resulting eight strips of land six
miles wide are called *ranges*. They are numbered
RANGES. both east and west, beginning at the principal meridians. The last range in the
southeastern part of the State is numbered "xviii.
east," and in the extreme western part the numbers reach "lvii. west." *Base lines* are parallels
of latitude used as standards. Such a line for the
surveys in Kansas and Nebraska is the fortieth
parallel, the common boundary between the
BASE
LINES. two states. North of this, at intervals of
GUIDE
PARAL- twenty-four miles, other lines are sur-
LELS.
veyed called *guide parallels*, the intervening land being divided into strips six miles wide.
The ranges are thus cut into squares measuring
six miles on the side, which are numbered northward in every range, beginning at the
CON-
GRES- southern boundary. They are called *con-*
SIONAL
TOWN- *gressional townships*, or sometimes, *geo-*
SHIPS.
graphical townships, to distinguish them
from organized townships. The whole State,
except on the large rivers, would be divided into
townships of uniform size if the meridians were
parallel. But they converge as they approach the
poles. On this account corrections have to be
made in the north and south lines, and some irregular pieces of land are formed, which are called
fractional townships. These lines fixed by the

government are not only of use in locating land,
but they serve quite an important purpose in dividing the State into uniform districts for purposes of

6	5	4	3	2	1
7	8	9	10	11	12
18	17	16	15	14	13
19	20	21	22	23	24
30	29	28	27	26	25
31	32	33	34	35	36

FIG. 2. NUMBERING OF SECTIONS IN A TOWNSHIP.

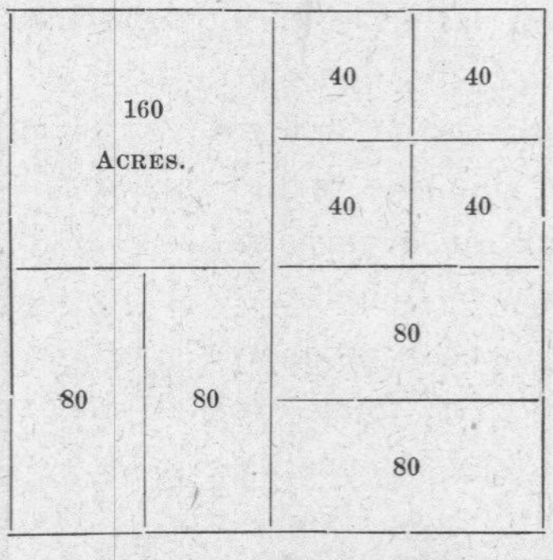

FIG. 3. ONE SECTION, WITH MINOR DIVISIONS.

administration.   People of the country districts
MINOR are familiar with the *section*, made by
DIVI-
SIONS. still further dividing the township by
lines one mile apart, and with the minor

divisions called *"quarter section," "eighty,"* and *"forty."*[1]

SUGGESTIVE TOPICS AND QUESTIONS.

1. Are all principal meridians numbered? See *Encyclopedia* at word *principal meridian.*

2. Locate a piece of land described as follows: W ½ of N E ¼, Sec. 16, T. 4 N., R. 7 West.

3. Where in a section would a farm be if described as S W ¼ of N E ¼? E ½ of S W ¼? N ½ of S E ¼?

---

[1] The manner of designating land by means of these lines is simple. T. 10 N., R. 2 E. means the tenth township north (of the base line) in the second range east (of the sixth principal meridian). A "W" instead of an "E" changes the location to one of the ranges west of the principal meridian. After the particular township is designated, in which a piece of land lies, the section is indicated by number, and the part of a section is shown by quarters or halves. Thus N W ¼ would be north-west quarter, and S ½, south half, etc.

II.—THE SCHOOL DISTRICT.

The kind of organization with which students generally are best acquainted, except in cities and villages, is the school district. It is formed by the county superintendent, upon a petition from the people affected by the change. Unless there is some special reason for it, a district contains not **FORMA-** less than four square miles of land, and **TION.** extends not more than six miles in any one direction. A school district, indeed, need not all be in one county, if the residents have presented the necessary petitions to the superintendents of the two counties. There are about seven thousand of these small districts in the state.[1] They are very irregular, each being formed according to the desire of the people con-**SHAPE.** cerned, or according to the situation with regard to rivers and streams.

All the people of the district are taken together as one body, of which the name is "*The School District No. . . . .of . . . . .County.*" Like the county and the state, it is treated in law as one person, and is distinguished from an individual by being called a *legal person.* When a number **A COR-** of persons are so organized into one body **PORA-** **TION OR** as to be able to hold property which be-**LEGAL** **PERSON.** longs to all alike, and to sue in the courts, it is then called a *corporation.* Just as

[1] In 1892.

a bank corporation elects officers to represent it and to carry on the work for which it is organized, so the school district has its officers to represent it and to do the work connected with the schools.[1]

The district acts as one body at its annual meeting. It is not essential to its character as a corporation that all the individual members meet in one place. The county and the state are corporations, but a meeting of all the members of either would seldom be possible. In re-

ANNUAL MEET-ING. spect to its coming together to do business, the school district reminds the student of the cities of Greece and Rome, in which all the citizens met in an open air assembly to make laws for the community. The annual meeting of each school district is held at the schoolhouse on the last Monday of June. Here the legal voters transact the business of the district. Who are the legal voters and what may be done at one

LEGAL VOT-ERS. of these assemblies? Any person of either sex over twenty-one years of age, who owns either real estate in the district or personal property that was taxed in his name at the last assessment, or who has school children in the district, is entitled to vote. All matters that come before the district at the annual meeting are connected with education. The most important power is the right to fix the amount of school tax. In a school district, as well as any-

---

[1] The Supreme Court has decided that a school district is only a sort of corporation.

where else in the state organization, the power
PUR-POSES OF THE DIS-TRICT. to take money is guarded with great care. The district elects three officers to represent it. These three, moderator, director, and treasurer, form a kind of committee known as the *school board.* The moderator presides at all meetings of the district, the treasurer cares for all money, and the director acts as a secretary of the district. They are best known **SCHOOL BOARD.** as the district school board, of which the director is the most important officer. He is a sort of chairman. The board looks after all things immediately connected with the school, **Powers and Duties.** such as hiring teachers, buying supplies, grading the school, and caring for the school building. Another important duty lately (1891) given to the board is the purchase **Care of Books.** and care of school books.[1] The power to own property belongs to all kinds of legal persons, or corporations.

Not all school districts are of the same grade. When a district has one hundred and fifty school children, it may become a high school district, if the majority of the voters so decide at the

---

[1] *Consolidated Statutes,* 1891 §§ 3758–3767. "District school boards, and boards of trustees of high school districts, and boards of education in cities of the first and second class, are hereby empowered and it is made their duty to purchase all text-books necessary for the schools of such district." A board may make contracts with publishers for a term of years, not over five, to purchase books at the lowest price at which they are sold. Parents can purchase books from the board at cost. A local dealer may be designated to handle the books, with some increase in price on account of handling and transportation.

annual meeting.   This change increases to six
HIGH SCHOOL DISTRICTS. the number on the school board, which annually elects from its members a moderator, director and treasurer.   A district of
this kind may vote to establish a high school.
Every city, sometimes with surrounding land attached, forms a school district. Cities having from
CITY SCHOOL DISTRICTS. 1,500 to 10,000 inhabitants have a board of six trustees, like the high school district, but they are elected in a different manner.
There is no "annual meeting" in a city, and the
members of the board are chosen at the regular
election.   In cities of the first class[1] nine members are elected for terms of three years.   Metropolitan cities have school boards of fifteen
Boards. members, of whom five are chosen each year.   When the board of a city organizes,
it elects a president, vice-president and secretary.   A city school board itself estimates the
Tax. amount of the school tax, while in the high school and·country districts the voters, instead of the board, fix the amount of the tax.

SUGGESTIVE TOPICS AND QUESTIONS.

1.   Make a map of your own school district.
2.   Look up derivation of word *corporation* in a dictionary.
3.   Is there more reason why women should be allowed to vote on school matters than on other subjects?
4.   What advantages and disadvantages arising from a school district owning all books used in a school?

---

[1] For classes of cities, see p. 86, Note.

III.—CITIES AND VILLAGES.

Scattered about over the State are more than three hundred cities and villages. These, too, are legal persons. Since the term *municipal* is applied to such collections of people, they may also be called *municipal corporations.* The classes[1] **MUNICI- PAL COR- PORA- TIONS.** of these are determined for the most part by population. Yet there is much freedom of choice. A thickly settled community does not have to form any such organization at all. It may remain a country district, governed as a part of the county, and being a corporation, perhaps, only as a school district. A village or city may constitute an entire school district. In that case it is both a school corporation for education and a municipal corporation for government and administration. The school district of the city is often larger than the municipality, some of the adjacent land being added.

The law-making part of a village consists of a

---

1 Inhabitants required for each class:
1.—*Village.*   *Consolidated Statutes*, 1891, §§ 2861–2963.
    (*a*)   200 to 1,500.
    (*b*)   Over 1,500, if adopted by the people.
2.—*Cities of Second Class. Statutes,* §§ 2721–2859.
    (*a*)   1,000–25,000.   (*Session Laws,* 1885, p. 156.)
    (*b*)   5,000–25,000.
3.—*Cities of First Class. Statutes,* §§ 2483–2720.
    (*a*)   10,000 to 25,000.
    (*b*)   25,000 to 100,000.
4.—*Metropolitan Cities. Statutes,* §§ 2368–2482.
    Over 80,000.

board of five trustees elected annually. The chairman of this board somewhat resembles the mayor of a city. The powers of the board extend

THE VIL- LAGE. to all subjects connected with preserving the peace and good order of the village, but they include also the appointment of officers that are usually elected in cities. Among these are clerk and treasurer. Violations of the ordinances of the village, as well as of the laws of the State, are tried before a justice of the peace belonging to the precinct in which the village is. Thus the village really has no separate judicial department. Likewise in the election of county and state officers and in the collection of taxes, it is a mere district of the county.[1]

Cities of the several classes have some features in common. A city always has a mayor, who is

THE CITY. chief officer and executive head. The body that makes the laws is in all cases the council, although it varies in number and power. It is usually made up of two members from each ward

Wards. or district of the city. Metropolitan cities have from six to ten wards, and smaller cities from two to six. In some cases[2] only one coun-

---

[1] Village Organization:

1.—*Board of Trustees:* (a) Number, five; (b) elected by voters; (c) officers are (1) chairman and (2) clerk, who is city clerk; (d) powers are very numerous, and extend to all matters connected with the welfare of the village. (*Consolidated Statutes*, 1891, §§2867, 2892-2900); these include taxation, and licensing or prohibiting selling and giving away liquor.

2.—*Village Officers:* (a) clerk; (b) treasurer; (c) overseer of streets; (d) marshal. All appointed by board of trustees. Terms, one year. Salaries, $150 to $300.

[2] In metropolitan cities and smaller cities of the first class.

cilman is chosen from a ward, and other councilmen
Coun-
cil.
equal in number to those representing particular wards are chosen by the whole city
without reference to districts.   Those not representing wards are called councilmen *at large* to distinguish them from the others.   All classes of
Elect-
ive
Officers.
cities agree in electing mayor, clerk, treasurer, and police judge.   Further than
this the classes do not agree.   In a large
city the number of minor executive officers is
very great.[1]   Some are appointed by the mayor
directly, others are appointed by the mayor and

---

1 Metropolitan cities:

1 *Area:* Not over 25 square miles.

2. *Wards:* Number, 6 to 10; each divided into election districts if
containing over 400 legal voters; each election district is a precinct of
the county.

3. *City elections:* (*a*) Held on the first Tuesday after the first Monday in Nov. 1891, 1893, 1895, etc.   Officers elected: mayor, treasurer,
comptroller, city clerk, and police judge.   See chapter on elections.

4. *Council:* (*a*) Membership: one from each ward and an equal number from the city at large. Bond $5,000. (*b*) Powers and duties: more nu-
merous as the city becomes larger. Council and mayor levy taxes. For
general purposes, not over 14 mills to the dollar. Council sits as a board of
equalization to adjust the taxes of the city. Special taxes may be levied
for sewers, paving, or any authorized public improvements. Among
other purposes are fire, light, and police. Appointments made by mayor
and council together: engineer, attorney, city prosecutor, street commissioner, inspector of buildings, boiler inspector, three members of
board of public works, etc.

5. *Executive officers:* (*a*) Mayor: appointing power in connection
with the council; has superintending control of all officers and affairs of
the city; enforces the laws of the city; recommends measures for "improvement of finances, police, health, security, ornament, comfort, and
general prosperity of the city." (*b*) City Clerk: term two years. (*c*)
Treasurer: receives and pays out money for city and keeps account of it;
term two years; must give bond for $200,000; is collector of the city
taxes. (*d*) Comptroller: general financial officer of the city.

6. Boards: (*a*) Council as a board of equalization. (*b*) Board of
public works. (*c*) Board for inspection of buildings. (*d*) Park commissioners: Five members appointed by the judges of the judicial district
in which the city is.   Term, five years.

council together, and still others are elected **Other Officers.** by the people. There is much difference of opinion about the amount of power that should be given to the mayor. Usually his power and responsibility are small, and many **Should the Power of the Mayor be Great?** things which he might look after are done by committees or "boards." In cities of the first class, like Lincoln, there are several of these committees, such as the board of public works, board of health, and excise board. It is now strongly urged that a mayor be given control of city government more completely, and made more responsible for the manner in which the business of the city is done. The reasons for this are many, one being that a single officer acts more promptly and systematically than a committee. A still stronger ground is a belief that the chances for corruption are less when the power and responsibility of the mayor are great.[1]

The police judge is the judicial part of the municipality. There are justices of the peace, it is true. In metropolitan cities six are elected. Yet the justices' court is a county institution, while the police judge is a city office.

SUGGESTIVE TOPICS AND QUESTIONS.

1. Derivation of words *municipal, ward, city, village,* and *mayor.*
2. May a city be a county? Look up the character of the city of London.
3. Why does a city need more rules and regulations than a country district?
4. If you live in a city or village, make a complete diagram of its government as it actually exists.

[1] See John Fiske, *Civil Govt.*, Chap V., Sec. 3, especially pp. 124–136.

IV.—THE COUNTY.

The question "Why do we have counties?" probably would be most frequently answered by saying that they are merely districts taken for convenience. But, in truth, counties exist in Nebraska because older states had this form.

REASON FOR COUNTIES. The officers of the Territory so divided it for a similar reason. It appears that originally in England a county, or *shire*, was not one of the divisions of a state, as now, but it existed under another name before the kingdom was formed. It was an "isolated tribal state" of the old Saxons. Small kingdoms were first formed by the union of these tribal units. A long period of conflict and growth resulted in larger groups, until at last all the small states were banded together under one name. "Scholars are now agreed that the first English shires were merely the old tribal states, each bearing a new and common name. As if in recognition of their nationality, of their equal rank and power, each of the latter was called a shire or *share* of the new commonwealth."[1] Officers and assemblies belonging to the several districts before their union, have been changed little by

ANTIQUITY. little, until now there are left only a few traces of their original character. The course of this development has been long, commenc-

---

[1] G. E. Howard, *Introd. to Local Const. Hist. of U. S.*, I., 299.

ing far back in the time of early England. A careful study on this subject must be made elsewhere.[1] There is barely room in this book to notice what the old shire has developed into. After being transplanted into the colonies, the county system has been adopted all over the United States with the progress of settlements westward.

THE TWO COUNTY SYSTEMS. Two distinct forms of organization have resulted, known as the *commissioner system* and the *supervisor system.* In the first form, the main feature is a board composed of commissioners, elected in districts of the county, each for a term of three years. The other plan is to have the county divided into townships, in each of which a supervisor is elected. Each supervisor represents his town in the county board, which thus becomes a representative assembly instead of a committee. The laws of Nebraska permit a county to adopt either of these forms.[2]

In this State the board of county commissioners is intrusted with all the important business interests of the people, such as roads and

---

[1] G. E. Howard, *Local Const. Hist.,* I. 289–473.

John Fiske, *Civil Govt. of U. S.,* Chap. III., pp. 48–95.

Jesse Macy, *Our Government,* Chap. II., 13–19.

[2] "The first type prevails in the great majority of states and territories, and * * * has descended in direct line from the colonial laws of Pennsylvania through those of the Northwest Territory, Ohio, Indiana, and Illinois,—to be variously modified by the legislation of recent times. The second type exists in a small group of states:" New York, Michigan, and Wisconsin; Illinois since 1849; Nebraska since 1883. It began by a law of the New York Assembly in 1703. Howard, *Local Const. Hst.,* I., 438–9.

bridges, support of the poor, and taxation. The **COMMIS-SOINER SYSTEM.** county is a corporation and the board acts for it in every instance. Officers at the county seat, or capital, cannot easily reach each neighborhood, and for that reason it is pro-**POWER OF THE BOARD.** vided that they shall divide the county into convenient districts. What could be more natural than that the board should make use of the geographical township for these divisions called **PRE-CINCTS.** *precincts?* This is what is usually done. In sparsely settled places a precinct may be made up of four townships, or it may even be smaller than a township where the population is dense. But in general it corresponds to the geographical township. The precincts are not legal persons at all. They are merely units for the transaction of local business. They do not even have meetings such as a school district has. They are necessary on account of the large area included in a county, some districts being far re-moved from the seat of government. The ancient assembly of the shire, the *scirgemot*, would be im-possible now. In county elections the voters of a precinct cast their ballots at a place in the precinct designated by the county board, from which the ballots are sent to the county seat. At **PRE-CINCT OFFI-CERS.** the same time that county officers are elected, the people of a precinct choose minor officers, whose duties lie wholly in their own district. Such are two justices of the peace, two constables, three judges and two clerks of election, and one assessor. Justices **ROAD DISTRICT.** of the peace and constables hold office for two years, but the others for one. There are usually four road districts in a precinct, for **COMMISSIONER DISTRICTS.** each of which an overseer of the highway is chosen. The precincts are grouped together to form commissioner districts, which elect a commissioner every three years.[1]

Although the power of the commissioners is quite extensive, there are many things that they cannot attend to. Other officers, county judge, **COUNTY OFFICERS.** sheriff, coroner, treasurer, clerk, surveyor, and county superintendent, share the work. Their powers and duties may be briefly summarized as follows: the judge may hear cases that are ordinarily tried before the justice of the peace, and civil cases not involving over $1,000 that may come before the district **THEIR DUTIES.** court. His is the *probate court*, which has exclusive right to try cases concerning wills, property of deceased persons, and guardianship of minors, insane persons and idiots. The sheriff executes the orders of the courts and arrests violators of the law. Perhaps it is not necessary to specify the duties of treasurer, clerk and surveyor, but those of the coroner are somewhat pe-

---

[1] In Nebraska one or two counties only have five commissioners. There are as many districts as there are officers of this kind to elect, the elections being so arranged that not all are chosen in one year. In the case of three districts, one election occurs each year, but in a different district. Where the population of the county is from 70,000 to 125,000, the commissioners are elected by a vote of the entire county. Otherwise they are voted for only by the electors of the district from which they come. *Consol. Statutes*, 1891, § 898.

culiar. As the person who investigates all cases of
death, presumed to be by unlawful means, by holding a coroner's inquest, he is the survival of the
old "crowner," whose business was to inquire into
wreckage, destructive fires, and sudden deaths.
The county superintendent, of course, has charge
of the school work. His duties embrace exami-
nation of persons wishing to teach, laying out
boundaries of school districts, and visiting every
school in the county at least once a year. He is
subject to the rules of the state superintendent.
The schools of a city are not under his supervision.

On the other hand, if a county adopts the supervisor system, or *township organization* as it is
SUPERVI-SOR SYSTEM. called, the scope of the county government is much more limited. The inter-
est of the people is more closely drawn to
local affairs. Precincts are only districts of the
county, and the power is all at the county seat.
Such a government is said to be centralized. In
TOWNS. the other form, the county is divided into
towns[1] or townships. Here, as in the case of
the precincts, the geographical division of six
miles square is largely followed. Every one of
these towns is a corporation, with a special name.
Every city of over 6,000 inhabitants constitutes a

[1] The word *town* is commonly used in the west for a small village,
but there are numerous uses besides. (See *Webster's International
Dictionary* or *Century Dictionary*.) It is used here to mean only the
township under the supervisor system. This is the meaning of the
word in the *Consol. Statutes of Nebraska, 1891*, and prevails altogether
in New England. See etymology of the word.

separate town. The voters hold an annual town meeting on the first Tuesday in April, and special meetings when called. Much of the work done by the commissioners is disposed of under the other system by the citizens at their annual meeting, such as supervision of roads and bridges. Even in the case of township organization, however, the county bears the expense of costly bridges. At the annual meeting the citizens tax themselves for all the necessary purposes of self-government, and elect their officers,[1]

SUPER-VISOR. the most important of whom is the supervisor. The clerk, justice of the peace and supervisor constitute the town board, which meets three times each year to examine the accounts of the

TOWN BOARD. town. The supervisors of all towns compose the county board, so called whether made up of commissioners or of supervisors. The county board meets semi-annually, two-thirds of the number constituting a quorum. The representation of the towns in the county board is a revival of a right which the *tunscipe*, or township of Anglo-Saxon times, had in the shire.

SUGGESTIVE TOPICS AND QUESTIONS.

1. Derivations and meanings: *Shire, precinct, probate, town.*
2. Is township organization successful? What points of disadvantage?

---

[1] Town clerk, town treasurer, three judges and two clerks of election, assessor, one overseer of highways for each road district, with annual terms. Two justices of peace and two constables, with terms of two years. In cities and villages, one additional supervisor for every 4,000 inhabitants.

V.—THE STATE.

The citizen of the school district is not only a member of the precinct and county, or of the township and county, as the case may be, but he also belongs to the greater corporation called the **PLACE OF A CITIZEN.** *State of Nebraska.* The number of districts[1] to which he belongs, one within the other, is confusing. Nevertheless it is his duty to know what his place is within the Commonwealth and the Nation. According to the democratic theory, in which American es- **THEORY OF DEMOCRACY.** pecially believe, the rights which kings and emperors have, belong to the people themselves. In a little democracy where the people all meet to discuss their affairs, there is no need of any representatives. But here it is manifestly impossible to get along without them. Although the powers of government belong to the voters, they may be delegated to a fewer

---

[1] (1) Road Districts.
(2) School District.
(3) Town.
(4) Commissioner District.
(5) County.
(6) Representative District.
(7) Senatorial District.
(8) Judicial District.
(9) United States Land District.
(10) Congressional District.
(11) United States Judicial District.
(12) Circuit of U. S. Judicial System.

number to exercise. This explains why voters
DELE-GATION OF POWERS. do not make laws, while they possess the power. The first step in build-
ing a state is to adopt a written statement of
principles and form of government. Not only
is such a document drawn up by men
ADOPTION OF A CONSTITUTION. elected for this particular purpose, but
when it is completed the people them-
selves adopt or reject it. Sometimes
a state repeats this process several times before
it is satisfied. Such a writing not only out-
lines the system, showing what officers there
shall be and of how many members the legislature shall be composed, but it also prescribes
minutely how each part shall be organized, and
how each officer shall perform his duty, and regulates very carefully the manner of making
laws. With this to be followed, the people may
safely intrust the public interest to chosen men,
only providing penalties for a betrayal of the
trust.

It may be well to notice a very interesting
fact before beginning a study of the constitution
of Nebraska. The earliest written constitutions
STATUTORY LAW IN CONSTITUTIONS. contained only the most general statement of principles.[1] They did not go be-
yond the limits of what is termed "constitutional." But gradually there crept into
them more and more of matters formerly left to
legislatures. This means that the people wish to

[1] On written constitutions, see John Fiske, *Civ. Govt.*, 187-196.

7

put many important subjects of legislation beyond
the reach of the legislature. Constitutions,
containing the supreme law in a state, have now
come to be very long, some of them covering
scores of pages in the statute books.

I.—CONSTITUTIONAL STUDIES: THE FRAME OF GOVERNMENT.

[In Appendix I., at the end of this book, the constitution
of Nebraska is to be found. It is placed there to use. The
following topics are intended to aid the student in studying
its provisions. The language of that instrument is plain,
and a student will seldom fail to understand it, as far as his
vocabulary goes. Certainly there are words to study, but
that is just what every scholar does all his life. *Webster's
International Dictionary*, or some other complete work of
the kind, should be within reach. Notes are added, explain-
ing some of the more difficult points. No attempt has been
made to repeat what there is in the constitution. The judgment of the teacher should decide the amount to be discussed
at a lesson, for not only are the topics of different importance, but the recitation period varies in different schools.]

A.—PERSONAL RIGHTS GUARANTEED BY THE CONSTITUTION.[1] Art. I.

1. Inherent Rights. Art. I., §§ 1, 26.
2. Object of Government. § 1.
3. Slavery. § 2.
4. Freedom of Conscience. § 4.
5. Freedom of Speech and of the Press. § 5.
6. Trials by Jury. §§ 6, 10–13.
7. Search and Seizure. § 7.

---

[1] The idea of putting a *Bill of Rights* into a constitution has descended to newer states from the original thirteen. It is largely a
statement of the rights denied to the colonists by Great Britain.

8. *Habeas Corpus.*[1] § 8.
9. Bail, Fines, and punishments. § 9.
10. Treason. § 14.
11. Penalties: *Corruption of Blood; Forfeiture; Transportation.*[2] § 15.
12. Relation of Military and Civil power. §§ 17, 18.
13. Right to Assemble. § 19.
14. Right of Petition. § 19.
15. Penalty for Debt. § 20.
16. Right of Property.[3] §§ 21, 25, 3.
17. Right to Vote: *Franchise.* § 22.
18. Right of Appeal, Error,[4] etc. § 24.

B.—DISTRIBUTION OF POWERS. Art. II.

C.—LEGISLATURE. Art. III.

1. Number of Houses. § 1.

---

[1] A writ is in the form of a letter stamped with an official seal. It is addressed by a court to a person, commanding something to be done or not to be done. *Habeas Corpus* means "you may have the body." The writ of this name is directed to an officer in whose charge a person is, bringing the prisoner before a certain court, in order to test the legality of his imprisonment.

[2] These three are old English penalties. Formerly, in case of high crimes, not only was the offender punished, but his descendents also. The taint that once attached to an offender for the commission of a felony in England, deprived him and his descendents of the right to inherit and transmit property. This taint is called *corruption of blood.* A *forfeiture* was the penalty by which the state deprived one of his property. Transportation suggests the Russian exile system, by which political prisoners are banished far into the interior of Siberia. Such a penalty is entirely foreign to the spirit of American institutions.

[3] The right of the government to appropriate the property of a citizen for public use is called the right of *Eminent Domain.*

[4] Section 23, Article 1., secures a right of some importance. The word *error* refers to mistakes in judicial proceedings, that would take away some right from the person being tried. A *writ of error* issues from a court of review to a lower court, commanding a case to be brought before the court of review. The writ of error is a personal right guaranteed by the constitution, like other personal rights.

---

[1] *Committee of the whole:* A name given to the whole senate, or house of representatives, acting as a committee. By this means the members secure more freedom in discussion, not being subject to the same rules as under the more formal organization. When a house "goes into committee of the whole," the presiding officer names a chairman. Upon arising the committee can only recommend, like any other committee; but because all members took part, a house usually adopts the report.

6. Powers of the Legislature and of each House. §§ 7, 9, 14; Art. V., § 4.

7. Prohibitions upon Legislation. §§ 15, 18, 21; Art. I., 16.[1]

8. Appropriation Bills. §§ 19, 22.

9. When are Laws in Force? § 24.

10. Publication of Laws. § 24.

D.—Executive. Art. V.

1. Term. § 1.

2. Qualifications. §§ 2, 3, 25.

3. Election returns. § 4.

4. Governor:—

Powers and duties. §§ 6–15, 20; Art. VI., § 21.

Succession to office in case of vacancy. §§ 16, 18.

5. Lieutenant Governor. §§ 16, 17.

6. Board of Public Lands and Buildings. § 19.

7. Reports and Accounts of Minor Officers. §§ 21, 22.

8. Seal of the State: In whose keeping? § 23.

9. Salaries. § 24.

E.—Judiciary. Art. VI.

1. Supreme Court:—

Number, term, qualification, etc., of judges. §§ 2–7, 13, 14.

Reporter, state librarian. § 8.

Jurisdiction.[2] § 2.

---

[1] An *ex-post-facto* law is one made to apply to cases arising before its enactment.

[2] *Original jurisdiction* in a case is the power to hear and determine it from the beginning.

2.   District Court:—
    Districts. §§ 10, 11.
    Number, term, etc., of judges. §§ 11,
        14.
    Jurisdiction : what cases can it try ? § 9.[1]
3.   County Court :—
    Term, etc., of judge.   § 15.
    Nature and jurisdiction of the court;
        special jurisdiction. § 16. See
        above, p. 93.
4.   Justice of the Peace, and Police Magis-
        trates. § 18.
5.   Appeals.   § 17.
6.   General Provisions.[2] §§ 17, 19, 22, 23.

As the State grows in wealth and numbers, changes in the laws are required. Not only do demands for legislation arise from this cause and from special circumstances in the State, but a **LEGIS-** spirit of improvement revises old ideas **LATION.** and calls for new and better things. Such a change was made by the Australian ballot law enacted in 1891, a reform measure adopted largely throughout the United States. Between real necessity for legislation and schemes of members who have axes to grind, the time of the legislature is fully occupied. It is fair to say that the work is seriously done, on the whole. Yet there

---

1 *Chancery*, from English Chancellor, a judicial officer. Chancery means the same as equity. Cf. *Consol. Statutes*, 1891, § 4538.

2 The Board of Transportation constitutes a sort of court. It is composed of attorney general, secretary of state, auditor, treasurer, commissioner of public lands and buildings, assisted by three secretaries. *Consol. Statutes*, 1891, §§ 597 ff.

are several points in which the work might be criticised. A common feature of politics in the **LOBBY-** legislature is *lobbying*. Bills rarely pass **ING AND LOG-** both houses of the legislature on their **ROLL- ING.** merits alone, but are engineered through by the skill of some interested person or persons. *Log-rolling* also largely prevails, a term applied to trading votes, where A agrees to vote for a bill in which B is interested, if B will support a measure for which A is working.

The growth of the importance of committees in law-making is more noticeable, perhaps, in Con- **WORK** gress than in the state legislatures, yet **BY COM- MIT-** it is coming to be a great feature of **TEES.** them also.

Students have learned from the constitution[1] that a census of the inhabitants may be made every ten years, beginning with 1885, and that after these enumerations, as well as after each Federal census, the members of the legis- **APPOR- TION-** lature may be apportioned among the **MENTS.** counties. The thirty-three senators and one hundred representatives are elected from these districts. Their arrangement is subject to frequent change and need not be dealt with in detail. It is a general fact of much interest, that with these and with the congressional dis- **GERRY-** tricts, most of the *gerrymandering* oc- **MAN- DERING.** curs.[2] This kind of fraud consists in a careful arrangement of districts, in such a

---

[1] Art. III. § 2.
[2] Fiske, *Civ. Gov.*, 216.

way as to give the dominant political party the advantage. Instead of districts of uniform shape, form is not considered at all. By a republican legislature, a democratic precinct, city, or county is frequently placed in a district in such a way that its majority is counterbalanced by other votes. Formerly this device was not much opposed, either party practicing it when opportunity offered. Lately, however, people are discussing the subject and apportionments are carefully watched.

The governor is not to the state what the president is to the United States. The latter is really **THE EX-ECUTIVE.** the head of his department. Secretary of state, secretary of treasury, etc., are subordinates to him. Not so with the governor. Instead of the head, he is merely a portion of the executive department. His co-workers **POSI-TION OF THE GOV-ERNOR.** are elected along with him, and owe him nothing, except as the law prescribes. Nevertheless the governor represents the State in its dealings with other states. Much of the executive work is now performed by bodies that are really permanent committees. The board of public lands and buildings[1] is as important as any of these bodies, having, in fact, general su-**STATE BOARDS** pervision and control of all the public lands and buildings in the State, except those devoted to educational purposes. Hardly less important, is the state board of equalization,

---

[1] Constitution, Art. V., § 19.

connected with the revenue system.[1] On account of the importance of the railroads in commerce, the board of transportation[2] may be named along with those already given. Also may be mentioned the board of school lands and buildings,[3] the board of health,[4] and the state printing board.[5]

THE JU-DICIARY. Each of the district judges is allotted to a district, as in the case of the members of the legislature. Nearly every one of these divisions have several counties, and its judge holds court at stated times in every county comprehended within its limits. **DIS-TRICTS.** The grouping of counties for this purpose is temporary, but the last apportionment (1891) is given in Map VI., p. 106, to illustrate all such arrangements.

CHAR-ACTER. The subject of the courts and what they do is a large one. It is short to say that the judges interpret the laws which the legislature makes, but there is not space enough in this book to mention the subjects of discussion connected with the department. It is important to know that this is the most reliable and permanent part of the state organism. It changes least and is made up of the most able men.

SUGGESTIVE TOPICS AND QUESTIONS.

1. Why are bills relating to finance allowed to originate only in the house of representatives?

---

[1] Below, p. 109.
[2] See p. 102, note 2.
[3] Constitution, Art. V., § 1.
[4] Governor, Attorney General, and Supt. of Pub. Inst.
[5] Auditor, Treasurer, Sec. of State.

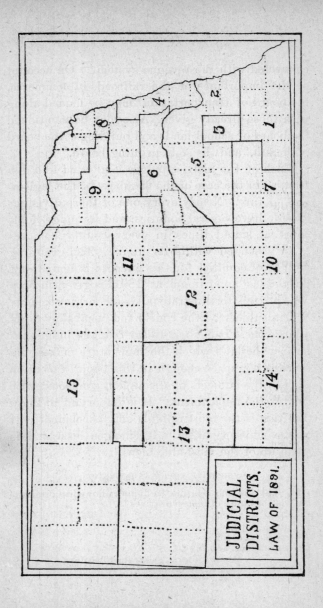

JUDICIAL DISTRICTS.
LAW OF 1891.

2. How do senatorial and representative districts compare in size?

3. Are bills of rights needed now in state constitutions?

4. What benefits arise from a separation of the functions of government into three departments?

5. Give instances where one department has powers belonging to another. See constitution, Art. III., § 14; Art. V., § 15.

6. What is a *seal of state* for?

7. Has there been any *gerrymandering* in Nebraska?

8. Is the tendency now to enlarge or to decrease the number of officers in the State?

9. Is the tendency to collect the powers into the hands of fewer officers, or to separate and specialize the duties?

10. May a district judge hold court out of his own district?

II.—TAXATION.

In the administration of government there remain three subjects of great interest. The one of these that most closely concerns the citizens of the state, is taxation. In the mind of the ordinary citizen the process by which he is taxed is vague and far away, except the terrible reality of taxes. The system in Nebraska, at least, is not complicated, and may be easily understood by giving the subject a little attention. The main idea involved is a simple problem in percentage. The people of the State have property, a certain **TAX IS A PERCENTAGE.** fractional part of which may be taken each year to defray the expenses of government. Certain officers of each State, county and lower division estimate the amount that will be needed for the next year. The problem is simply this: Given the amount from which to raise the tax and the amount of tax needed; to find the rate. Divide the percentage by the base, and the result is the rate of taxation for the next year.

The manner of finding each item, however, may not be clear.   What kinds of property may be taxed, and how does the State know the amount of it?   In regard to the first question, the laws of the State name four kinds.   First, all real and personal property; second, all moneys, credits, bonds, or stocks, and other investments, the shares of stock of companies and associations and all other personal property, including property on the way to or from this State, if the owner lives in Nebraska; third, the shares of bank stock, if the banks are doing business in this State; fourth, the capital stock of companies organized under the laws of Nebraska.   The process of valuation begins with the assessor of each precinct or township.   The first step is the annual meeting of the assessors of the county at the office of the county clerk, on the third Tuesday of March.   The purpose is to fix the value of the various kinds of property to be assessed.   The blanks which the assessor of a precinct or township uses are provided by the auditor of public accounts. They pass through the hands of the county clerk, who fills in the lists of lands and lots to be assessed.   The assessor visits every part of his district between April 1st and June 1st, and values all taxable property of each person.   The books are returned to the county clerk, and in the early part of June the county board hold a meeting, at which they review

TAXA-BLE PROP-ERTY.

VALUA-TION.

ASSES-SOR.

BOARDS OF EQUAL-IZA-TION.

the work of the assessors. The board is said to sit as a *board of equalization* at this time, because it equalizes the values in the several districts. In metropolitan cities and cities of the first class, the council sits as a board of equalization. Those who think their lands valued too high may complain to the county board, or city council, while it is sitting as such a board. In this manner the valuation of the property in a county is corrected, and justice is done to all, as nearly as possible. These boards fix the rates for the county and for the city.

Not only is this equalization made in each county, but the governor, auditor and treasurer form a board to adjust the values in the **STATE BOARD OF EQUAL-IZA-TION.** State as a whole. They examine the various county assessments, and if it appears to them that the valuation has not been made with reasonable uniformity in different counties, they adjust matters by varying the rate of taxation, instead of changing the values of property. This state board of equalization, having before it the valuation of taxable property in the state, proceeds to find the rate for the several **STATE FUNDS.** amounts to be raised. There is the general State tax, the sinking fund tax, and the school tax. Each of these or any other special fund to be raised, is divided by the whole valuation to find the rate. After the state and county boards have made all adjustments and the rate has been fixed, each county clerk makes out another list of the amounts due from every piece of taxable property, and delivers the list to the county treasurer, formally commanding him to **COLLECTION OF TAXES.** collect them. The law provides, however, that "no demand for taxes shall be necessary, but it shall be the duty of every person subject to taxation under the laws of the State to attend at the treasurer's office at the county seat and pay his taxes." In cities, the municipal taxes are paid into the city treasury. State funds are paid into the county treasury. All the county and state taxes are added and the **CONSOLIDATED TAX.** result is called the "consolidated tax." It even contains local levies for school purposes. Thus all the money for taxes, except in cities, comes into the county treasury, from which it is sent either to the state treasury or to the district for which it was collected.[1]

---

[1]Example of taxes in Nebraska for one year. A resident of Bennet had state, county, and village assessments. The city levy was paid by residents of Lincoln, besides county and state taxes.

STATE LEVY.	Mills.
General Fund	5.00
Sinking Fund	0.125
School Fund	0.5
University Fund	0.375
Inst. Feeble-Minded Fund	0.125
State Relief Fund	0.125
	6.25

COUNTY LEVY.	
General Fund	7.2
Road Fund	2.3
Bridge Fund	2.8
Sinking Fund	4.2
Insane Fund	0.9
Soldiers' Relief Fund	0.3
	17.7

VILLAGE LEVY.	Mills.
Bennet	10.
Firth	10.
Hickman	5.
Roca	10.
University Place	10.
West Lincoln	10.
Waverly	18.
Bethany Heights	10.
Capital and Midand Prec	10.

CITY LEVY.	
Interest and Coupon	5.
Water	1.
Police	0.3
Library	0.75
School	5.
Fire	0.4
General	18.
Sewer	2.
Water-Emergency	4.3
Judgment	1.5
Road	7.
Storm Water Sew'r J'dgm'nt.	5.25
Sinking Fund, Road Purposes	2.5

Besides these general taxes, there are other special assessments. Every male inhabitant of each road district between twenty-one and fifty years of age, is subject to pay a labor tax **SPE- CIAL TAXES.** of three dollars, which may be paid in cash or by work. It is called more commonly a poll tax. A village or city tax of the same kind takes the place of this road tax. In cities, especially, the number of different taxes multiply rapidly. Inhabitants of particular districts may be assessed for building and repairing sidewalks, for sanitary purposes, or for sprinkling the streets. **LI- CENSES.** Other charges are made under the name of licenses. These are usually levied to regulate some class of business, such as the sale of liquors. They are imposed not to raise money, primarily, but to regulate the sale of intoxicating drinks. So with the dog tax in cities. It is not to raise money, but to make owners responsible for the damage dogs may do. A tax upon peddlers appears to be levied, not so much for regulating the business, or for raising money, as to insure the fact that the peddler shall pay a tax somewhere in the State. All people who enjoy any of the protection and benefits of the State government, should aid in defraying its expenses.

There is always an effort on the part of the person whose property is being assessed, to have the value of his property placed as low as possible. The assessors, in turn, have generally estimated the value very low, and the result is that value of taxable property in the State has been much less than it should, and the rate of taxation much higher.   Nothing at all is gained by such low estimates, and a great deal is lost, for capital is prevented from coming into the State on account of the high rate.

SUGGESTIVE TOPICS AND QUESTIONS.

1. What advantages or disadvantages in a low valuation?

2. Is there any moral question involved in using saloon money for school purposes?

3. What power regarding revenue did the Continental Congress have? What result?

4. Problem: Valuation of property in a school district $18,000.00: money to be raised for a school building $540.00. Find the rate of the levy.

III.—ELECTIONS.[1]

The American people pride themselves upon the right to vote, for it is the power by which they govern themselves.   The system by which **ELECT-ORS.** the voters, or *electors,* of the State exercise this right in choosing their officers should be thoroughly understood by every citizen.   The first inquiry is, "Who are these *electors?*" as they are called in the statutes.   The constitution fully answers this, and students may refer to that document.[2]   The legislature has completed the first paragraph of Section 1, Article VII., by making it read, "in the county forty days, and in the precinct, township, or ward, ten days."[3]   There is no separate residence qualification for cities, ex-

---

[1] *Consol. Statutes,* 1891, §§ 1582–1778.

[2] Article VII.

[3] *Consol. Statutes,* 1891, § 1584.

cept for those of the first class, having more than 25,000 inhabitants. Here a voter must have resided three months. A clause of the Federal con-

CITIZENS. stitution provides that all persons born and naturalized in the United States and subject to its jurisdiction, are citizens of the United States and of the state in which they reside. The constitution of Nebraska provides that persons of a foreign birth who, thirty days before an election, shall have declared their intention to

ALIENS. become citizens, may be voters. This means that they shall have taken the first step in naturalization thirty days beforehand. The first step of a foreigner in acquiring citizenship is an application, in which he not only affirms that he wishes to become a citizen of the United States, but that he renounces all allegiance to the government to which he previously belonged. Criminals, persons of unsound mind, and

THOSE NOT VOTERS those belonging to the army and navy of the United States are not entitled to vote. The reasons are evident, at least in the case of the first two classes. It is clear, too, in regard to those in the employ of the United States, that if they could vote in any state where they happened to be, there would be a strong temptation for the authorities to place the soldiers where their votes would be most needed. Minors, or those under twenty-one years of age, are not permitted to vote, for reasons unnecessary to give.

8

Except in school matters, women, in Nebraska, have not yet obtained the franchise.

The next question that presents itself to the mind of the student is, "For whom do electors vote?" May a voter cast his ballot for any one to **CANDI-DATES.** fill a certain position? Nothing prevents him from so doing, but a regular process is prescribed in order that voting may be more orderly. Nominations for office are made (1) by convention or primary meeting, and (2) sometimes **TWO WAYS TO NOM-INATE.** by petition. The latter is a statement, or certificate of nomination, signed by voters. Five hundred are required if the office concerns all the voters of the State. For a county or smaller district, only fifty are required. A convention or primary meeting is any "organized assemblage of voters or delegates" that represents some political party. The system of party nominations varies somewhat according to the needs of the party, but the general plan is as follows: Each particular district has a central committee. Chief in the State is the *state central committee.* When there is need for a state convention, this body issues a call to similar organizations in the counties. Each of these in turn brings together the committee of every ward. Arrangements are then **WARD CAUCUS.** made for a ward *caucus* of the party voters, which nominates delegates for a county convention, to be voted for at the party *primaries.* These are elections in which, according to law, only the members of the party may vote whose delegates are to be chosen. County conventions, **PARTY PRIMA-RIES.** thus formed from elected delegates, place men in nomination for county offices, or, in other words, make out the *ticket* for **THE TICKET.** the county. At the same time delegates are elected to go to the state convention. Such a body, representing the party of the State, sends men to the national party convention. The business of the inter-state body is to choose presidential candidates for the party, and to **VAR-IOUS CON-VEN-TIONS.** make a party platform. There are also conventions in the several representative, senatorial, judicial, and congressional districts, consisting of delegates elected at the county meeting. Altogether the system is by no means simple, and the parties do not always go through the formalities.

The questions that now remain to be answered are mainly concerned with the conduct of voters and the system of recording the election returns. **REGIS-TRA-TION.** In cities of more than 2,500 inhabitants there is a registration law in force, requiring voters to register on certain days before election. Three supervisors of registration are appointed by the council for each election district in a city.[1] On one of the registration days[2]

---

[1] Qualifications of supervisors are stated somewhat minutely in the law. The three must be of at least two political parties; citizens of good character and voters of the precinct in which they serve; able to read, write, and speak the English language intelligently; and not candidates for any office concerned in the election in which they are supervisors.

[2] "Tuesday four weeks, the Wednesday of the third week, the Thursday of the second week, and the Friday and Saturday of the first week preceding the day of the November election of each year."

a voter should have his name, place of residence, date and place of birth, citizenship, etc., recorded. Otherwise, on election day he must get a certificate of citizenship from the city clerk and have it signed by two freeholders of the district in which he lives.   Except in cities, registration is not necessary.

Up to a recent date voting has been open to such endless frauds that even with great care an honest election was not often secured. **OLD ELECTION LAW.** Scenes at elections under the old law are still fresh in the minds of Nebraskans: challengers at the window on either side of a long line of voters, each awaiting his turn to cast a ballot; ticket peddlers by the score; electioneering on every hand, and withal an atmosphere suggesting the opposite of order, square dealing, and good citizenship. Election carousals are a thing of the past. By the new ballot law of 1891, a marvelous change has come over the character of election day. Now electioneering must not be carried on within one hundred feet of the **AUS- TRA- LIAN BALLOT LAW.** election place. Saloons are closed. The ballot box is removed from the window to a room fitted out with compartments, stalls or booths. Each of these is supplied with desk, pens, and ink, and so arranged that the voter may not be watched as he marks his ballot. A rail encloses the writing compartments, so that no one outside of it can come within twelve feet of them.[1]   The

[1] Six feet in country districts on account of small rooms.

number of voters in each election district is restricted to three hundred, and one booth is required for every fifty.

In each precinct three judges and two clerks of election are chosen, and in cities where registration is required, two additional judges. The judges designate two of their number to hand ballots to the voters. Every ballot must be signed by two judges before it is handed out. Two kinds of ballots are required to be printed. *Sample ballots* are made and given out six days before election, so that any one may see that they are correct. They must be on green or red paper, not on white. *Official ballots*, on the other hand, are only on white paper, and no one but the county clerk may print them. They must be ready in his office at least four days before election. The number of ballots that are sent to each voting place is recorded, and when the ballots are returned after election, there must be the same number. A voter has no ballot before he is given one by a judge, and under no circumstances is he permitted to take one from the room. Upon receiving it he goes to one of the unoccupied booths and there marks an X opposite the name of candidates for whom he wishes to vote. If a ballot is spoiled he may have as many as four, but each must be returned to the judges before another is received. The names of candidates are arranged alphabetically under each office, like the following:

KINDS OF BALLOTS.

MARKING A BALLOT.

FOR COUNTY TREASURER.	VOTE FOR ONE.
(Mr. A.)	Independent |
(Mr. B.)	Prohibition |
(Mr. C.)	Democrat |
(Mr. D.)	Republican |

FOR SHERIFF.	VOTE FOR ONE.
(Mr. A.)	Prohibition |
(Mr. B.)	Republican |
(Mr. C.)	Democrat |
(Mr. D.)	Independent |

When the voter has completed the marking, he must fold the ballot so that nothing shall appear on the outside except the signature of the judges.

Every precaution is thus taken to secure secrecy in voting. After the polls are closed the first thing the judges are required to do is to compare the poll books and correct mistakes until **COUNT-** the books agree. Then the ballot boxes **ING** **THE** are opened and the ballots counted with- **VOTES.** out being unfolded. In case the number of ballots exceeds the number of persons voting, the ballots are put back into the box, shaken up, and enough drawn out to make the number of voters and ballots the same. The canvass must be public. The several kinds of ballots are made into separate packages and sealed, each being marked "ballots cast," "ballots rejected," or "spoiled and unused ballots." And all are sent to the county clerk, who makes within six days an abstract or complete statement of the vote

from all the precincts. The votes for most of the
state officers[1] are canvassed by the legislature, but
those cast for presidential electors are counted by
a *state board of canvassers,*[2] consisting of governor, secretary, auditor, treasurer, and attorney
general. In case of a tie in the number of votes
for an officer of a county or some smaller district,
the two parties involved decide the matter by
drawing lots at the county court house.

SUGGESTIVE TOPICS AND QUESTIONS.

1. Derivation and meaning of *alien, franchise, caucus,
precinct, canvass.*
2. Origin of Australian Ballot system: *Review of Re-
views,* III., 609, July, 1891.
3. Should the right to vote be restricted by requiring
an educational test?
4. Is there any *property qualification* for voters in the
United States?
5. What is *residence?* If one's business is in a different
precinct or ward from his family, where does he vote? May
a state or county officer vote where he resides temporarily
two years on account of his office?

IV.—EDUCATION.

Mention has been made of the land set apart by
the organic law for the maintenance of the schools.
SCHOOL LANDS. The whole amount of land devoted to this
purpose is more than two and one-half
millions of acres.[3] Two sections out of every

---

[1] Votes canvassed by legislature are those cast for governor, lieutenant governor, members of Congress, secretary of state, auditor of
public accounts, state treasurer, state superintendent of public instruction, attorney general, commissioner of public lands and buildings, and district attorneys; also votes expressing choice of people for
United States Senator.

[2] State board canvasses votes for presidential electors, judges of
supreme and district courts, and regent of university.

[3] Number acres set apart in sections 16 and 36 in each township:
2,733,500.

township in the State is a magnificent endowment
for the common schools. Likewise the State has
endowed its normal school and university.[1] The
wealth thus set apart is never diminished, the interest only being used. When school lands are
leased, the rent forms a part of the fund. From
this source alone the revenue is not sufficient.
The districts tax themselves for local school pur-
OTHER poses, according to the length of term,
MEANS
OF SUP- number of teachers, cost of school build-
PORT. ing, etc., desired.[2] The State levies an
additional tax yearly for educational purposes,
but this may not exceed one and one-half mills.
Besides this there are various fines and licenses
that are paid into the general fund. Here are
four sources of revenue. It is natural to inquire
at this place how much this amounts to in a year.
COST OF During the school year ending with July,
SCHOOLS. 1891, the total expenditure for the common schools was over four million dollars, one-
half of which was paid to teachers.[3]

At the head of the school system is the state
superintendent, who is recognized as the leader in
the work and the interpreter of the school laws
of the State, and whose decision is authority,
unless reversed by the courts. Next below him
comes the county superintendent, who may be

---

[1] Normal school, 12,804 acres.

  University, 134,566 acres.

[2] Limited to twenty-five mills on a dollar of valuation.

[3] Total expenditure, $4,123,799,54. Cost of hiring teachers, $2,116,-
668,58. Buildings, etc., $749,632.89.

said to be the manager of the county schools.
STATE AND COUNTY SUPER-IN-TEND-ENTS. His duties of laying out districts, visiting the schools, and holding institutes make him the center of that school system. Above the common schools are the two higher institutions, the normal school and the university.

NOR-MAL SCHOOL. The first of these is mainly for the purpose of fitting students to be teachers.[1] On the other hand, the state university is intended to give a student the choice of many courses, in order to fit him to be a useful citizen **UNI-VER-SITY.** and servant of the State.[2] The unity of the whole plan of free education is its important feature. Every part is made to work

---

[1] *State Normal School* at Peru :—

1.—Superintended by board of education, consisting of state treasurer, state superintendent, and five others appointed by the governor for terms of five years each. Board elect president and secretary.
2.—Managed by a principal, who is responsible for the condition of the school.
3.—Completion of common school course of study entitles a student to a diploma good for two years. Completion of higher course of study and a certain amount of teaching after graduation entitles a student to a life certificate.
4.—Tuition free.

[2] *State University* at Lincoln :—

1.—Governed by a board of regents. (See *Constitution*, Art. VIII., Sec. 10.)
2.—Departments provided for:
    (*a*) College of literature, science, and art.
    (*b*) Industrial college, embracing agriculture, practical science, civil engineering, and the mechanic arts.
    (*c*) College of law.
    (*d*) College of medicine, only preparatory course having been established.
    (*e*) College of fine arts.
3.—Tuition free and advantages open to all without regard to sex or color.
4.—Summer school for teachers is held.
5.—"University Extension" affords instruction to the public through lectures.

in harmony with the rest. The university and the normal school may be called public schools as well as the lower grades.

V.—PUBLIC INSTITUTIONS.

Not only does the State offer education generously to its citizens, but it extends its protection and care to the unfortunate. It is thus that the necessity arises for what the law calls charitable and

CARE FOR SPECIAL CLASSES. penal institutions. The blind are offered a home and free instruction at the Institute for the Blind at Nebraska City. Here they are taught the rudiments of an English education and music, and instruction is also given in several trades, such as broom making, basket making, piano tuning, etc. The deaf and dumb are

PART OF THE EDUCATIONAL SYSTEM. offered similar advantages at the institute at Omaha. The feeble-minded youth of the State are also offered a home and instruction at the institution located at Beatrice. At all these institutions, which are as purely educational as the university and normal school, instruction is given in accordance with the highest scientific authority. Not only is the instruction free, but a good home is offered. Furthermore when any of these wards are unable to provide proper clothing or to pay railroad fare, the authorities of the institutions are authorized to provide for such cases and charge the same to the county from which the ward comes.

The industrial or reform schools of the State—

the one for boys at Kearney and the one for girls at Geneva—should also be classed as educational institutions. Those children who refuse to receive instruction offered at home, and who show by their conduct that they are likely to become bad citizens, are sent by local authorities to these schools.

Here they are given an elementary education in the English branches and are taught useful trades, being treated in such a way as usually to develop honor and industry. This is all done at the expense of the State, for the purpose of raising the standard of useful citizenship.

OBJECT TO RAISE THE STANDARD OF CITIZENSHIP.

The purpose of the home for women at Milford, and the home for the friendless at Lincoln, are also in the line of raising the standard of morals and adding to the ranks of good citizens. At the latter institution, orphaned and friendless children are received, cared for, and provided with good homes.

There is a growing idea that a penitentiary also should be for reform, rather than for discipline. Be that as it may, the influence upon the convicts of learning trades must result in more or less education. It is even proposed to establish a school within the penitentiary. Insane hospitals are too frequently mere places of confinement. It is a benefit to the public to have the State care for the insane, but it is charity to them to be treated as patients, not as convicts.

IDEA OF A PENITENTIARY.

Although these public institutions cannot be sharply classified, yet a general analysis may be made as follows:—

(a)—EDUCATIONAL.

1. State Industrial or Reform Schools,
    (1) for boys, at Kearney.
    (2) for girls, at Geneva.
2. Institution for the Deaf and Dumb, at Omaha.
3. Institution for Feeble-minded Youth, at Beatrice.
4. Institution for the Blind, at Nebraska City.

(b)—CHARITABLE.

1. Soldiers' and Sailors' Home, at Grand Island.
2. Milford Home for Women, at Milford.
3. Home for the Friendless, at Lincoln.
4. Insane Hospitals,
    (1) at Lincoln.
    (2) at Norfolk.
    (3) at Hastings, for incurable insane.

(c)—PENAL.

1. State Penitentiary, at Lincoln.

VI.—FEDERAL RELATIONS.

The Federal government is almost a stranger to the every day life of the people. The common dealings of men have to do with the State. **POWERS OF THE U. S.** Nevertheless the United States has obtained some important rights under the constitution which was adopted in 1788. Besides the powers that belong to a government dealing with other nations, powers necessary to its support, such as taxation, are conferred upon it. No insignificant amount of revenue is collected in this State every year for the United States government.[1] Usually the most manifest evidence of the power of a nation is its military. The power which a European nation shows to other governments or to its own people, is an extensive army and navy. This is not true of the United States, which has relied very little on its army and navy to retain its place among the nations or its control over its own territory. How, then, does the power of the United States appear in Nebraska? Probably its ever-present author-

[1] During the years from 1880 to 1890 the following amounts of internal revenue have been collected from Nebraska and Dakota, 1880–1883 being from Nebraska alone, and the remainder coming from Nebraska and the two Dakotas.

1880...........$ 912,784.86	1884...........$1,515,816.43	1888...........$2,778,269.38
1881............ 962,064.86	1885............ 1,971,269.12	1889............ 2,248,624.19
1882............ 1,108,191.15	1886............ 1,674,013.12	1890............ 2,969,745.17
1883............ 1,320,517.24	1887............ 2,393,404.70	

ity is nowhere seen so well as in its courts. Not
FEDERAL only does the State of Nebraska have a
COURTS. system of courts, but the Federal government also maintains one or more courts in each
state. Nebraska is concerned with only one
of the nine circuits into which the states are
grouped.[1] Every state in this eighth circuit except
three, forms one Federal judicial district, in which
a judge holds court. A circuit court is held in
each district by one of the two circuit judges
which are appointed. In his absence the district
judge may open circuit court and hear cases that
belong to it, at the same time that district court is
in session. Formerly there were only the three
courts of the United States with which a state was
concerned, the district, the circuit, and the supreme
court. Lately (1891) a new court has been established in each circuit, called the circuit court of
appeals. It is held at St. Louis for the eighth circuit. Three judges compose this court. The
circuit justice, who is the United States supreme
court judge assigned to the eighth circuit, together
with the two circuit judges, may constitute
CIR-
CUIT the appeal court. If one or more of these
COURT
OF AP- is away, a district judge may take his
PEALS.
place. Special district judges are designated for this purpose. Before the establishment
of this new court, the decision of a circuit court

---

[1] The eighth circuit now (1892) embraces Arkansas, Iowa, Missouri,
Colorado, Kansas, Minnesota, Nebraska, North Dakota, South Dakota,
Wyoming, Indian Territory, New Mexico, Oklahoma, and Utah.

was final, except in cases involving over $5,-000. Above this cases could be taken to the supreme court. The new circuit court of appeals has authority to hear any case that has been tried in the lower courts of the United States, but cases involving more than $5,000 may be carried to Washington.

**JURIS-
DIC-
TION.**

Among the Federal administrative officers in Nebraska, the district attorney is the business agent of the Nation. In any matter arising in connection with mail, revenue or commerce, he represents the central government and acts for it in all suits. In any case concerning the amount of duty on imports or concerning national banks, the district attorney is counsel for the United States. The post office, which involves a great deal of traffic, is under the immediate control of an executive officer. The laws governing it, however, are made by congress. The post office system has developed under the care of the Nation. From the postmaster general, in the cabinet, down to the least clerk in a country post-office, there are a very large number of employees, who were formerly appointed by the president, the post-master general, and his subordinates. Now, however, a far better plan has been introduced. It opens the positions to competition, and provides examinations for applicants. This plan, known as the *civil service* movement, is a step in removing the "spoils"

**ADMINIS-
TRATIVE
BUSINESS.**

**DIS-
TRICT
ATTOR-
NEY.**

**POST
OFFICE.**

system, or the system of rewarding partisans with

CIVIL SER- VICE RE- FORM.
office. Beginning with the most impor- tant clerkships in the executive depart- ment, it has been gradually extended to the lower positions and also to other de- partments of the government.

Many students have already heard about the "Original Package" bill. This involves the fact

COM- MERCE.
that the United States has control of all commerce between states. When a case arises concerning goods carried from one state to another, it must come before the United States courts. In connection with commercial relations, it is pertinent to ask what is meant by

PORTS OF ENTRY.
Lincoln and Omaha being *ports of entry.* Not all customs that are levied upon goods brought into this country are col- lected at the harbor or place where the goods en- ter our boundaries. In order that the goods may not have to be unpacked and packed again, the United States establishes custom houses in the interior, where all imports may be inspected and taxed according to the laws of congress. The places where such custom houses are located are called ports of entry.

Since the first grants of land to the Union Pa- cific railroad during the territorial period, many thousands of acres of land have been given for the same purpose. The United States has taken such a part in starting these great projects as

public highways, that the question has arisen
RAIL-ROADS. whether the Nation ought not to own
them. Railroads carry so much freight
and are used so extensively for traveling that they
are of more than state importance. Nevertheless
the State attempts to regulate the charges for
freight and passengers, by the board of transportation.

Another subject of importance which the Nation controls is the banking system. The laws of
Nebraska regulate how the business may be carried on here, but national banks are
NA-TIONAL BANKS. formed under the laws of the United
States. Among the advantages of the
system are great security for depositors and uniformity in bank notes.

The state shares in the national government
through its representatives. Every state is entitled
CON-GRESS. to have two in the senate and as many in
the house as its population entitles it to.
have. The senators represent the states as
SENA-TORS. equal units, but in the house the number
from each state is according to popu-
lation. The number of people which one congressman represented at the beginning of
REPRE-SENTA-TIVES. the national government in 1788 was 30,-
000. Now it has increased to 173,901.
The grouping of counties for the six districts are
shown in the accompanying map. Although a
congressman is chosen in the autumn, his term of
office does not begin until the following March 4.

9

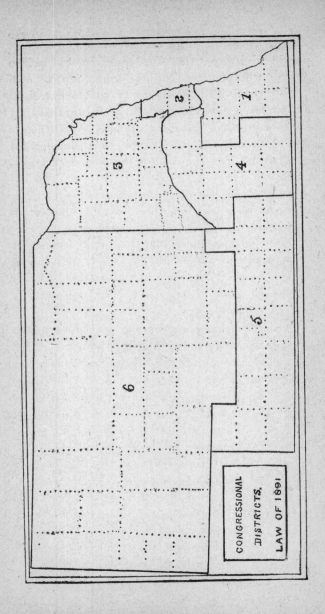

CONGRESSIONAL DISTRICTS, LAW OF 1891.

Usually, however, congress does not meet until the December after that, so that it is a year from the time a representative is elected before he has a chance to take his seat.

APPENDIX I.

CONSTITUTION OF NEBRASKA.

ADOPTED 1875.

PREAMBLE.

We, the people, grateful to Almighty God for our freedom, do ordain and establish the following declaration of rights and frame of government, as the constitution of the State of Nebraska:

ARTICLE I.—BILL OF RIGHTS.

SECTION 1. All persons are by nature free and independent, and have certain inherent and inalienable rights; among these are life, liberty, and the pursuit of happiness. To secure these rights, and the protection of property, governments are instituted among people, deriving their just powers from the consent of the governed.

SEC. 2. There shall be neither slavery nor involuntary servitude in this State, otherwise than for the punishment of crime, whereof the party shall have been duly convicted.

SEC. 3. No person shall be deprived of life, liberty, or property, without due process of law.

SEC. 4. All persons have a natural and indefeasible right to worship Almighty God according to the dictates of their own consciences. No person shall be compelled to attend, erect, or support any place of worship against his consent, and no preference shall be given by law to any religious society, nor shall any interference with the rights of conscience be permitted. No religious test shall be required **RELI-GIOUS FREE-DOM.** as a qualification for office, nor shall any person be incompetent to be a witness on account of his religious belief; but nothing herein shall be construed to dispense with oaths and affirmations. Religion, morality, and knowledge, however, being essential to good government, it shall be the duty of the legislature to pass suitable laws to protect every religious denomination in the peaceful enjoyment of its own mode of public worship, and to encourage schools and the means of instruction.

SEC. 5. Every person may freely speak, write, and publish on all subjects, being responsible for the abuse of that liberty; and in all trials for libel both civil and criminal, the truth, when published with good motives and for justifiable ends, shall be a sufficient defense.

SEC. 6. The right of trial by jury shall remain inviolate, but the legislature may authorize trial by a jury of a less number than twelve men, in courts inferior to the district court.

SEC. 7. The right of the people to be secure in their persons, houses, papers, and effects against unreasonable searches and seizures, shall not be violated; and **SEARCH AND SEIZURE.** no warrant shall issue but upon probable cause, supported by oath or affirmation, and particularly describing the place to be searched and the person or thing to be seized.

SEC. 8. The privilege of the writ of habeas corpus shall not be suspended, unless, in case of rebellion or invasion, the public safety requires it and then only in such manner as shall be prescribed by law.

SEC. 9. All persons shall be bailable by sufficient sureties, except for treason and murder, where the proof is evident or the presumption great. Excessive bail shall not be **BAIL.** required, nor excessive fines imposed, nor cruel and unusual punishments inflicted.

SEC. 10. No person shall be held to answer for a criminal offense, except in cases in which the punishment is by fine or imprisonment, otherwise than in the penitentiary, in case of impeachment, and in cases arising in the army and **CRIMINAL OFFENSES.** navy or in the militia, when in actual service in time of war or public danger, unless on a presentment or indictment of a grand jury; *Provided,* That the legislature may, by law, provide for holding persons to answer for criminal offenses on information of a public prosecutor, and may by law abolish, limit, change, amend, or otherwise regulate the grand jury system.

SEC. 11. In all criminal prosecutions the accused shall have the right to appear and defend in person or by counsel, to demand the nature and cause of accusation, **IMPARTIAL TRIAL.** and to have a copy thereof; to meet the witnesses against him face to face; to have process to compel the attendance of witnesses in his behalf, and a speedy public trial by an impartial jury of the county or district in which the offense is alleged to have been committed.

SEC. 12. No person shall be compelled, in any criminal case, to give evidence against himself, or be twice put in jeopardy for the same offense.

SEC. 13. All courts shall be open, and every person, for any injury done him in his lands, goods, person or reputation, shall have a remedy by due course of law, and justice administered without denial or delay.

SEC. 14. Treason against the State shall consist only in levying war against the State, or in adhering to its enemies,

TREA-SON. giving them aid and comfort. No person shall be convicted of treason unless on the testimony of two witnesses to the same overt act, or on confession in open court.

SEC. 15. All penalties shall be proportioned to the nature

PENAL-TIES. of the offense, and no conviction shall work corruption of blood or forfeiture of estate; nor shall any person be transported out of the State for any offense committed within the State.

SEC. 16. No bill of attainder, *ex post facto* law, or law impairing the obligation of contracts, or making any irrevocable grant of special privileges or immunities, shall be passed.

SEC. 17. The military shall be in strict subordination to the civil power.

SEC. 18. No soldier shall, in time of peace, be quartered in any house without the consent of the owner; nor in time of war, except in the manner prescribed by law.

SEC. 19. The right of the people, peaceably to assemble to consult for the common good, and to petition the government or any department thereof, shall not be abridged.

SEC. 20. No person shall be imprisoned for debt in any civil action, *mesne* or final proceedings, unless in cases of fraud.

SEC. 21. The property of no person shall be taken or damaged for public use without just compensation therefor.

SEC. 22. All elections shall be free; and there shall be no hindrance or impediment to the right of a qualified voter to exercise the elective franchise.

SEC. 23. The writ of error shall be a writ of right in all cases of felony; and in capital cases shall operate as a supersedeas to stay the execution of the sentence of death until the further order of the supreme court in the premises.

SEC. 24. The right to be heard in all civil cases in the court of last resort, by appeal, error, or otherwise shall not be denied.

SEC. 25. No distinction shall ever be made by law between resident aliens and citizens in reference to the possession, enjoyment, or descent of property.

SEC. 26. This enumeration of rights shall not be construed to impair or deny others retained by the people, and all powers not herein delegated remain with the people.

ARTICLE II.—DISTRIBUTION OF POWERS.

SECTION 1. The powers of the government of this State are divided into three distinct departments: the legislative, executive, and judicial, and no person, or collection of persons, being one of these departments, shall exercise any power properly belonging to either of the others, except as hereinafter expressly directed or permitted.

ARTICLE III.—LEGISLATIVE.

SECTION 1. The legislative authority is vested in a senate and house of representatives.

SEC. 2. The legislature shall provide by law for an enumeration of the inhabitants of the State in the year eighteen hundred and eighty-five, and every ten years thereafter; and at its first regular session after each enumeration, and also **CENSUS.** after each enumeration made by the authority of the United States, but at no other time, the legislature shall apportion the senators and representatives according to the number of inhabitants, excluding Indians not taxed and soldiers and officers of the United States army and navy.

SEC. 3. The number of representatives shall never exceed one hundred, nor that of senators thirty-three. The sessions of the legislature shall be biennial, except as otherwise provided in the constitution.[1]

SEC. 4. The terms of office of members of the legislature shall be two years, and they shall each receive for their ser- **TERM OF OFFICE AND COMPENSATION.** vices three dollars for each day's attendance during the session, and ten cents for every mile they shall travel in going to and returning from the place of meeting of the legislature on the most usual route; *Provided, however,* That they shall not receive pay for more than forty days at any one session; and neither members of the legislature nor employees shall receive any pay or perquisites other than their pay per diem and mileage.

SEC. 5. No person shall be eligible to the office of senator or member of the house of representatives, who shall not be **QUALIFICATIONS.** an *elector*, and have resided within the district from which he is elected for the term of *one year next* before his election, unless he shall have been absent on the public business of the United States, or of this State. And no person elected as aforesaid shall hold his office after he shall have removed from such district.

SEC. 6. No person holding office under the authority of the United States, or any lucrative office under the authority of this State, shall be eligible to or have a seat in the legislature; but this provision shall not extend to precinct or township officers, justices of the peace, notaries public, or officers of the militia; nor shall any person interested in a contract with, or an unadjusted claim against the State, hold a seat in the legislature.

---

[1] First half omitted. It applied to legislature only before 1880.

SEC. 7. The session of the legislature shall commence at twelve o'clock (noon) on the first Tuesday in January, in the year next ensuing the election of members thereof, and at no other time, unless as provided by this constitution. A majority of the members elected to each house shall constitute a quorum. Each house shall determine the rules of its proceedings, and be the judge of the election returns, and qualifications of its members; shall choose its own officers; and the senate shall choose a temporary president to preside when the lieutenant-governor shall not attend as president, or shall act as governor. The secretary of state shall call the house of representatives to order at the opening of each new legislature, and preside over it until a temporary presiding officer thereof shall have been chosen and shall have taken his seat. No member shall be expelled by either house, except by a vote of two-thirds of all the members elected to that house, and no member shall be twice expelled for the same offense. Each house may punish by imprisonment any person, not a member thereof, who shall be guilty of disrespect to the house, by disorderly or contemptuous behavior in its presence, but no such imprisonment shall extend beyond twenty-four hours at one time, unless the person shall persist in such disorderly or contemptuous behavior.

TIME OF SESSION.

QUORUM.

ORGANIZATION.

SEC. 8. Each house shall keep a journal of its proceedings, and publish them (except such parts as may require secrecy), and the yeas and nays of the members on any question shall, at the desire of any two of them, be entered on the journal. All votes in either house shall be *viva voce.* The doors of each house and of the committee of the whole shall be open, unless when the business shall be such as ought to be kept secret. Neither house shall, without the consent of the other, adjourn for more than three days.

JOURNAL. PUBLICITY.

SEC. 9. Any bill may originate in either house of the legislature, except bills appropriating money, which shall originate only in the house of representatives, and all bills passed by one house may be amended by the other.

SEC. 10. The enacting clause of a law shall be, " Be it enacted by the Legislature of the State of Nebraska," and no law shall be enacted except by bill. No bill shall be passed unless by assent of a majority of all the members elected to each house of the legislature. And the question upon the final passage shall be taken immediately upon its last reading, and the yeas and nays shall be entered upon the journal.

ENACTING CLAUSE OF LAWS.

SEC. 11. Every bill and concurrent resolution shall be read at large on three different days in each house, and the bill and all amendments thereto shall be printed before the

vote is taken upon its final passage.   No bill shall contain
BILLS. more than one subject, and the same shall be clearly
expressed in its title. And no law shall be amended
unless the new act contains the section or sections so
amended, and the section or sections so amended shall be
repealed.   The presiding officer of each house shall sign, in
the presence of the house over which he presides, while the
same is in session and capable of transacting business, all
bills and concurrent resolutions passed by the legislature.

SEC. 12.   Members of the legislature, in all cases except
treason, felony or breach of the peace, shall be privileged
from arrest during the session of the legislature, and for fifteen days next before the commencement and after the termination thereof.

SEC. 13.   No person elected to the legislature shall receive
any civil appointment within this State, from the governor
and senate during the term for which he has been elected.
QUALI- And all such appointments, and all votes given for
FICA- any such member for any such office or appoint-
TIONS. ment, shall be void.   Nor shall any member of the
legislature, or any state officer, be interested, either
directly or indirectly, in any contract with the State, county,
or city, authorized by any law passed during the term for
which he shall have been elected, or within one year after the
expiration thereof.

SEC. 14.   The senate and house of representatives, in joint
convention, shall have the sole power of impeachment, but a
majority of the members elect must concur therein.   Upon
the entertainment of a resolution to impeach by either
house, the other house shall at once be notified thereof, and
the two houses shall meet in joint convention for the purpose
of acting upon such resolution within three days of such no-
tification.   A notice of an impeachment of any officer other
than a justice of the supreme court, shall be forthwith
served upon the chief justice by the secretary of the senate,
who shall thereupon call a session of the supreme court to
meet at the capital within ten days after such notice to try
the impeachment.   A notice of an impeachment of a justice
of the supreme court shall be served by the secre-
IM- tary of the senate upon the judge of the judicial dis-
PEACH- trict within which the capital is located, and he
MENT. thereupon shall notify all the judges of the district
court in the State to meet with him within thirty days at the
capital, to sit as a court to try such impeachment, which
court shall organize by electing one of its number to preside.
No person shall be convicted without the concurrence of two-
thirds of the members of the court of impeachment, but
judgment in cases of impeachment shall not extend further
than removal from office and disqualification to hold and en-
oy any office of honor, profit, or trust in this State, but the

party impeached, whether convicted or acquitted, shall nevertheless be liable to prosecution and punishment according to law. No officer shall exercise his official duties after he shall have been impeached and notified thereof, until he shall have been acquitted.

SEC. 15. The legislature shall not pass local or special laws in any of the following cases, that is to say:

For granting divorces.

Changing the names of persons or places.

Laying out, opening, altering, and working roads or highways.

Vacating roads, town plats, streets, alleys, and public grounds.

Locating or changing county seats.

Regulating county and township offices.

Regulating the practice of courts of justice.

Regulating the jurisdiction and duties of justices of the peace, police magistrates, and constables.

Providing for changes of venue in civil and criminal cases.

Incorporating cities, towns, and villages, or changing or amending the charter of any town, city, or village.

Providing for the election of officers in townships, incorporated towns, or cities.

Summoning or empaneling grand or petit juries.

Providing for bonding of cities, towns, precincts, school districts, or other municipalities.

Providing for the management of public schools.

Regulating the interest on money.

The opening and conducting of any election, or designating the place of voting.

The sale or mortgage of real estate belonging to minors or others under disability.

The protection of game or fish.

Chartering or licensing ferries or toll bridges.

Remitting fines, penalties, or forfeitures.

Creating, increasing, and decreasing fees, percentage, or allowances of public officers during the term for which said officers are elected or appointed.

Changing the law of descent.

Granting to any corporation, association, or individual, the right to lay down railroad tracks, or amending existing charters for such purpose.

Granting to any corporation, association, or individual, any special or exclusive privileges, immunity, or franchise whatever. In all other cases where a general law can be made applicable, no special law shall be enacted.

SEC. 16. The legislature shall never grant any extra compensation to any public officer, agent, servant, or contractor, **EXTRA COMPENSATION.** after the services shall have been rendered, or the contract entered into. Nor shall the compensation of any public officer be increased or diminished during his term of office.

SEC. 17. The legislature shall never alienate the salt springs belonging to the State.

SEC. 18. Lands under the control of the State shall never be donated to railroad companies, private corporations, or individuals.

SEC. 19. Each legislature shall make appropriations for the expenses of the government until the expiration of the first fiscal quarter after the adjournment of the next regular session, and all appropriations shall end with such fiscal quarter. And whenever it is deemed necessary to **APPRO-PRIA-TION.** make further appropriations for deficiencies, the same shall require a two-thirds vote of all the members elected to each house, and shall not exceed the amount of revenue authorized by law to be raised in such time. Bills making appropriations for the pay of members and officers of the legislature, and for the salaries of the officers of the government, shall contain no provision on any other subject.

SEC. 20. All offices created by this constitution shall become vacant by the death of the incumbent, by removal from **VACAN-CIES.** the State, resignation, conviction of a felony, impeachment, or becoming of unsound mind. And the legislature shall provide by general law for the filling of such vacancy when no provision is made for that purpose in this constitution.

SEC. 21. The legislature shall not authorize any games of chance, lottery, or gift enterprise under any pretense, or for any purpose whatever.

SEC. 22. No allowance shall be made for the incidental expenses of any state officer except the same be made by general appropriation and upon an account specifying each item. No money shall be drawn from the treasury except in pursuance of a specific appropriation made by law, and on the presentation of a warrant issued by the auditor thereon, **DRAW-ING MONEY.** and no money shall be diverted from any appropriation made for any purpose, or taken from any fund whatever, either by joint or separate resolution. The auditor shall, within sixty days after the adjournment of each session of the legislature, prepare and publish a full statement of all moneys expended at such session, specifying the amount of each item, and to whom and for what paid.

SEC. 23. No member of the legislature shall be liable in any civil or criminal action whatever for words spoken in debate.

SEC. 24. No act shall take effect until three calendar months after the adjournment of the session at which it **WHEN ACTS TAKE EFFECT.** passed, unless in case of emergency (to be expressed in the preamble or body of the act) the legislature shall, by a vote of two-thirds of all the members elected to each house otherwise direct. All laws shall be published in book form within sixty days after the adjournment of each session, and distributed among the several counties in such manner as the legislature may provide.

ARTICLE [IV.]—LEGISLATIVE APPORTIONMENT.

ARTICLE V.—EXECUTIVE DEPARTMENT.

SECTION 1. The executive department shall consist of a governor, lieutenant-governor, secretary of state, auditor of public accounts, treasurer, superintendent of public instruction, attorney-general, and commissioner of public lands and

OFFICERS OF EXECUTIVE DEPARTMENT. buildings, who shall each hold his office for the term of two years from the first Thursday after the first Tuesday in January next after his election, and until his successor is elected and qualified.[1] The governor, secretary of state, auditor of public accounts and treasurer shall reside at the seat of government during their terms of office, and keep the public records, books, and papers there, and shall perform such duties as may be required by law.

SEC. 2. No person shall be eligible to the office of governor or lieutenant-governor, who shall not have attained to the

QUALIFICATIONS. age of thirty years, and been for two years next preceding his election a citizen of the United States and of this State. None of the officers of the executive department shall be eligible to any other state office during the period for which they shall have been elected.

SEC. 3. The treasurer shall be ineligible to the office of treasurer for two years next after the expiration of two consecutive terms for which he was elected.

SEC. 4. The returns of every election for the officers of the executive department shall be sealed up and transmitted by the returning officers to the secretary of state, directed to the speaker of the house of representatives, who shall, immediately after the organization of the house, and before

ELECTION RETURNS. proceeding to other business, open and publish the same in the presence of a majority of each house of the legislature, who shall, for that purpose, assemble in the hall of the house of representatives. The person having the highest number of votes for either of said offices shall be declared duly elected; but if two or more have an equal and the highest number of votes, the legislature shall, by joint vote, choose one of such persons for said office. Contested elections for all of said offices shall be determined by both houses of the legislature, by joint vote, in such manner as may be prescribed by law.

---

[1] A temporary provision omitted, which also states that each election shall be held on Tuesday following the first Monday in November in even numbered years.

SEC. 5.   All civil officers of this State shall be liable to impeachment for any misdemeanor in office.

SEC. 6.   The supreme executive power shall be vested in the governor, who shall take care that the laws be faithfully executed.

SEC. 7.   The governor shall, at the commencement of each session, and at the close of his term of office, and whenever the legislature may require, give to the legislature information by message of the condition of the State, and shall recommend such measures as he shall deem expedient. He shall account to the legislature, and accompany his message with a statement of all moneys received and paid out by him from any funds subject to his order, with vouchers, and, at the commencement of each regular session, present estimates of the amount of money required to be raised by taxation for all purposes.

SEC. 8.   The governor may, on extraordinary occasions, convene the legislature by proclamation, stating therein the purpose for which they are convened, and the legislature shall enter upon no business except that for which they were called together.

SEC. 9.   In case of a disagreement between the two houses with respect to the time of adjournment, the governor may, on the same being certified to him by the house first moving the adjournment, adjourn the legislature to such time as he thinks proper, not beyond the first day of the next regular session.

SEC. 10.   The governor shall nominate and, by and with the advice and consent of the senate (expressed by a majority of all the senators elected voting by yeas and nays), appoint all officers whose offices are established by this constitution, or which may be created by law, and whose appointment or election is not otherwise by law or herein provided for; and no such officer shall be appointed or elected by the legislature?

SEC. 11.   In case of a vacancy during the recess of the senate, in any office which is not elective, the governor shall make a temporary appointment until the next meeting of the senate, when he shall nominate some person to fill such office; and any person so nominated, who is confirmed by the senate (a majority of all the senators elected concurring by voting yeas and nays), shall hold his office during the remainder of the term, and until his successor shall be appointed and qualified. No person, after being rejected by the senate, shall be again nominated for the same office at the same session, unless at request of the senate, or be appointed to the same office during the recess of the legislature.

SEC. 12.   The governor shall have power to remove any officer whom he may appoint, in case of incompetency, neg-

lect of duty, or malfeasance in office, and he may declare
his office vacant, and fill the same as herein provided in other
cases of vacancy.

SEC. 13. The governor shall have the power to grant re-
prieves, commutations and pardons after conviction, for
all offenses, except treason and cases of impeachment, upon
such conditions and with such restrictions and limitations
as he may think proper, subject to such regulations as may
be provided by law relative to the manner of applying for
pardons. Upon conviction for treason, he shall have power
to suspend the execution of the sentence until the case shall
be reported to the legislature at its next session, when the
legislature shall either pardon or commute the sentence, direct the execution of the sentence, or grant a further reprieve.
He shall communicate to the legislature, at every regular
session, each case of reprieve, commutation or pardon
granted, stating the name of the convict, the crime of which
he was convicted, the sentence and its date, and the date of
the reprieve, commutation or pardon.

SEC. 14. The governor shall be commander-in-chief of the
military and naval forces of the State (except when they
shall be called into the service of the United States), and
may call out the same to execute the laws, suppress insurrection, and repel invasion.

SEC. 15. Every bill passed by the legislature, before it becomes a law, and every order, resolution, or vote, to which
the concurrence of both houses may be necessary (except on
questions of adjournment), shall be presented to the governor. If he approve, he shall sign it, and there-

**VETO
POWER.** upon it shall become a law, but if he do not approve, he shall return it, with his objections, to the
house in which it shall have originated, which house shall
enter the objections at large upon its journal, and proceed
to reconsider the bill. If then three-fifths of the members
elected agree to pass the same, it shall be sent, together
with the objections, to the other house, by which it shall
likewise be reconsidered; and if approved by three-fifths of the
members elected to that house, it shall become a law, notwithstanding the objections of the governor. In all such
cases, the vote of each house shall be determined by yeas
and nays, to be entered upon the journal. Any bill which
shall not be returned by the governor within five days (Sun-
day excepted), after it shall have been presented to him,
shall become a law, in like manner as if he had signed it, unless the legislature by their adjournment, prevent its return;
in which case it shall be filed, with his objections, in the office
of the secretary of state within five days after such adjournment, or become a law. The governor may disapprove any
item or items of appropriation contained in bills passed by
the legislature, and the item or items so disapproved shall be

stricken therefrom, unless re-passed in the manner herein prescribed in cases of disapproval of bills.

SEC. 16. In case of the death, impeachment, and notice
thereof to the accused, failure to qualify, resignation, absence
from the State, or other disability of the governor, the powers, duties, and emoluments of the office for the residue of
the term, or until the disability shall be removed, shall devolve upon the lieutenant governor.

SEC. 17. The lieutenant governor shall be president of
the senate, and shall vote only when the senate is equally
divided.

SEC. 18. If there be no lieutenant governor. or if the lieutenant governor, for any of the causes specified in section
sixteen of this article, become incapable of performing the
duties of the office, the president of the senate shall act as
governor until the vacancy is filled, or the disability removed; and if the president of the senate for any of the above
named causes, shall become incompetent of performing the
duties of governor, the same shall devolve upon the speaker
of the house of representatives.

SEC. 19. The commissioner of public lands and buildings,
the secretary of state, treasurer, and attorney-general, shall
form a board, which shall have general supervision and control of all the buildings, grounds, and lands of the State, the
state prison, asylums, and all other institutions thereof, except those for educational purposes; and shall perform such
duties, and be subject to such rules and regulations, as may
be prescribed by law.

SEC. 20. If the office of auditor of public accounts, treasurer, secretary of state, attorney-general, commissioner of
public lands and buildings, or superintendent of public instruction, shall be vacated by death, resignation,
VACAN-CIES IN OFFICE. or otherwise, it shall be the duty of the governor to
fill the same by appointment; and the appointee
shall hold his office until his successor shall be
elected and qualified in such manner as may be provided by
law.

SEC. 21. An account shall be kept by the officers of the
executive department, and of all the public institutions of
the State, of all moneys received or disbursed by them severally from all sources, and for every service performed, and a
semi-annual report thereof be made to the governor, under
oath, and any officer who makes a false report shall be guilty
of perjury, and shall be punished accordingly.

SEC. 22. The officers of the executive department, and of
all the public institutions of the State, shall, at least ten days
preceding each regular session of the legislature, severally
report to the governor, who shall transmit such reports to
the legislature, together with the reports of the judges of the
supreme court, of defects in the constitution and laws, and

the governor, or either house of the legislature, may, at any time require information in writing, under oath, from the officers of the executive department, and all officers and managers of state institutions, upon any subject relating to the condition, management, and expenses of their respective offices.

SEC. 23. There shall be a seal of the State, which shall be called the "Great Seal of the State of Nebraska," which shall be kept by the secretary of state, and used by him officially, as directed by law.

SEC. 24. The salaries of the governor, auditor of public accounts, and treasurer, shall be two thousand five hundred ($2,500) dollars each per annum, and of the secretary of state, attorney-general, superintendent of public instruction, and commissioner of public lands and buildings, shall be two thousand ($2,000) dollars each per annum. The lieu-

SALA-RIES. tenant-governor shall receive twice the compensation of a senator, and after the adoption of this constitution they shall not receive to their own use any fees, costs, interest upon public moneys in their hands or under their control, perquisites of office or other compensation, and all fees that may hereafter be payable by law for services performed by an officer, provided for in this article of the constitution, shall be paid in advance into the state treasury. There shall be no allowance for clerk hire in the offices of the superintendent of public instruction and attorney-general.

SEC. 25. The officers mentioned in this article shall give bonds in not less than double the amount of money that

BONDS. may come into their hands, and in no case in less than the sum of fifty thousand dollars, with such provisions as to sureties and the approval thereof, and for the increase of the penalty of such bonds as may be prescribed by law.

SEC. 26. No other executive state office shall be continued or created, and the duties now devolving upon officers not provided for by this constitution shall be performed by the officers herein created.

ARTICLE VI.—THE JUDICIAL DEPARTMENT.

SECTION 1. The judicial power of this State shall be vested in a supreme court, district courts, county courts, justices of the peace, police magistrates, and in such other courts inferior to the district courts as may be created by law for cities and incorporated towns.

SEC. 2. The supreme court shall consist of three judges, a

SU-PREME COURT. majority of whom shall be necessary to form a quorum, or to pronounce a decision. It shall have original jurisdiction in cases relating to the revenue, civil cases in which the State shall be a party, man-

10

damus, quo warranto, habeas corpus, and such appellate
jurisdiction as may be provided by law.

SEC. 3. At least two terms of the supreme court shall be
held each year at the seat of government.

SEC. 4. The judges of the supreme court shall be elected
by the electors of the State at large, and their terms of office, except of those chosen at the first election, as hereinafter provided, shall be six years.

SEC. 5. The judges of the supreme court shall, immediately
after the first election under this constitution, be classified
by lot, so that one shall hold his office for the term of two
years, one for the term of four years, and one for the term of
six years.

SEC. 6. The judge of the supreme court having the shortest term to serve, not holding his office by appoint-
CHIEF JUSTICE. ment or election to fill a vacancy, shall be the chief
justice, and as such shall preside at all terms of the
supreme court; and in case of his absence, the
judge having in like manner the next shortest term to serve
shall preside in his stead.

SEC. 7. No person shall be eligible to the office of judge of
the supreme court unless he shall be at least thirty years of
age, and a citizen of the United States; nor unless he shall
have resided in this State at least three years next preceding
his election.

SEC. 8. There shall be appointed by the supreme court a
reporter, who shall also act as clerk of the supreme court,
and librarian of the law and miscellaneous library of the
state, whose term of office shall be four years, unless sooner
removed by the court, whose salary shall be fixed by law,
not to exceed fifteen hundred dollars per annum. The copy-
right of the state reports shall forever belong to the State.

· SEC. 9. The district courts shall have both chancery and
common law jurisdiction, and such other jurisdiction as the
legislature may provide, and the judges thereof may admit
persons charged with felony to a plea of guilty, and pass
such sentence as may be prescribed by law.

SEC. 10. [A temporary provision concerning the apportionment.]

SEC. 11. The legislature, whenever two-thirds of the members elected to each house shall concur therein, may, in or
after the year one thousand, eight hundred and eighty, and
not oftener than once in every four years, increase the number of judges of the district courts, and the judicial districts
of the State. Such districts shall be formed of compact territory, and bounded by county lines; and such increase, or
any change in the boundaries of a district, shall not vacate
the office of any judge.

SEC. 12. The judges of the district courts may hold courts
for each other, and shall do so when required by law.

SEC. 13. The judges of the supreme and district courts shall each receive a salary of $2,500, per annum, payable quarterly.

SEC. 14. No judge of the supreme or district courts shall receive any other compensation, perquisite, or benefit for or on account of his office in any form whatsoever, nor act as attorney or counsellor-at-law, in any manner whatever, nor shall any salary be paid to any county judge.

SEC. 15. There shall be elected in and for each organized county one judge, who shall be judge of the county court of such county, and whose term of office shall be two years.

SEC. 16. County courts shall be courts of record, and shall have original jurisdiction in all matters of probate, settlements of estates of deceased persons, appointment of guardi-**COUNTY** ans and settlement of their accounts, in all matters **COURT:** relating to apprentices, and such other juris-**JURIS-** diction as may be given by general law. But they **DICTION** shall not have jurisdiction in criminal cases in which the punishment may exceed six months imprisonment, or a fine of over five hundred dollars; nor in actions in which title to real estate is sought to be recovered, or may be drawn in question; nor in actions on mortgages or contracts for the conveyance of real estate; nor in civil actions where the debt or sum claimed shall exceed one thousand dollars.

SEC. 17. Appeals to the district courts from the judgments of county courts shall be allowed in all criminal cases on application of the defendant, and in all civil cases on application of either party, and in such other cases as may be provided by law.

SEC. 18. Justices of the peace and police magistrates shall be elected in and for such districts, and have and exercise such jurisdiction as may be provided by law; *Provided,* **JUS-** That no justice of the peace shall have jurisdiction **TICES** of any civil case where the amount in controversy **OF THE** shall exceed two hundred dollars, nor in a crimi-**PEACE.** nal case where the punishment may exceed three months imprisonment, or a fine of over one hundred dollars, nor in any matter wherein the title or boundaries of land may be in dispute.

SEC. 19. All laws relating to courts shall be general and of uniform operation, and the organization, jurisdiction, powers, proceedings, and practice of all courts of the same class or grade, so far as regulated by law and the force and effect of the proceedings, judgments, and decrees of such courts severally, shall be uniform.

SEC. 20. All officers provided for in this article shall hold their offices until their successors shall be qualified, and they **TERMS** shall respectively reside in the district, county, or **OF OF-** precinct for which they shall be elected or ap-**FICE.** pointed. The terms of office for all such officers, when not otherwise prescribed in this article, shall be two years. All officers, when not otherwise provided for in this article, shall perform such duties and receive such compensation as may be provided by law.

SEC. 21. In case the office of any judge of the supreme court, or of any district court shall become vacant before the expiration of the regular term for which he **VACAN-** was elected, the vacancy shall be filled by appoint-**CIES IN** ment by the governor, until a sucessor shall be **OF-** **FICES** elected and qualified, and such successor shall be **OF** elected for the unexpired term at the first general **JUDGES.** election that occurs more than thirty days after the vacancy shall have happened. Vacancies in all other elective offices provided for in this article shall be filled by election, but when the unexpired term does not exceed one year, the vacancy may be filled by appointment, in such manner as the legislature may provide.

SEC. 22. The State may sue and be sued, and the legislature shall provide, by law, in what manner and in what courts suits shall be brought.

SEC. 23. The several judges of the courts of record shall have jurisdiction at chambers as may be provided by law.

SEC. 24. All process shall run in the name of " The State of Nebraska," and all prosecutions shall be carried on in the name of "The State of Nebraska."

ARTICLE VII.—RIGHTS OF SUFFRAGE.

SECTION 1. Every male person of the age of twenty-one years or upwards, belonging to either of the following classes, who shall have resided in the State six months, and in the county, precinct, or ward, for the term provided by law, shall be an elector.

First. Citizens of the United States.

Second. Persons of foreign birth who shall have declared their intention to become citizens conformably to the laws of the United States, on the subject of naturalization, at least thirty days prior to an election.

SEC. 2. No person shall be qualified to vote who is *non compos mentis*, or who has been convicted of treason or felony under the law of the State, or of the United States, unless restored to civil rights.

SEC. 3. Every elector in the actual military service, of the United States, or of this State, and not in the regular army, may exercise the right of suffrage at such place, and under such regulations as may be provided by law.

Sec. 4. No soldier, seaman, or marine, in the army and navy of the United States, shall be deemed a resident of the State in consequence of being stationed therein.

SEC. 5. Electors shall in all cases, except treason, felony, or breach of the peace, be privileged from arrest during their attendance at elections, and going to and returning from the same, and no elector shall be obliged to do military duty on the days of election, except in time of war and public danger.

SEC. 6.   All votes shall be by ballot.

SECTION 1.   The governor, secretary of state, treasurer, attorney-general, and commissioner of public lands and buildings shall, under the direction of the legisla-

BOARD OF SCHOOL LANDS. ture, constitute a board of commissioners for the sale, leasing, and general management of all lands and funds set apart for educational purposes, and for the investment of school funds in such manner as may be prescribed by law

SEC. 2.   All lands, money, or other property, granted, or bequeathed, or in any manner conveyed to this State for educational purposes, shall be used and expended in accordance with the terms of such grant, bequest, or conveyance.

SEC. 3.   The following are hereby declared to be perpetual funds for common school purposes, of which the annual interest or income only can be appropriated, to-wit:

First.   Such per centum as has been, or may hereafter be granted by congress on the sale of lands in this State.

Second.   All moneys arising from the sale or leasing of sections number sixteen and thirty-six in each township in this State, and the lands selected, or that may be selected in lieu thereof.

Third.   The proceeds of all lands that have been or may hereafter be granted to this State, where, by the terms and conditions of such grant the same are not to be otherwise appropriated.

Fourth.   The net proceeds of lands and other property and effects that may come to the State, by escheat or forfeiture, or from unclaimed dividends, or distributive shares of the estates of deceased persons.

Fifth.   All moneys, stocks, bonds, lands and other property, now belonging to the common school fund.

SEC. 4.   All other grants, gifts, and devises that have or may hereafter be made to this State, and not otherwise appropriated by the terms of the grant, gift, or

TEMPO- RARY SCHOOL FUND. devise, the interest arising from all the funds mentioned in the preceding section, together with all the rents of the unsold school lands, and such other means as the legislature may provide, shall be exclusively applied to the support and maintenance of common schools in each district in the State.

SEC. 5.   All fines, penalties, and license moneys arising under the general laws of the State, shall belong and be paid over to the counties, respectively, where the same may be levied or imposed, and all fines, penalties, and license moneys arising under the rules, by-laws, or **FINES, PENAL-** ordinances of cities, villages, towns, precincts, or **TIES,** other municipal sub-divisions less than a county, **AND LI-** shall belong and be paid over to the same respect- **CENSE MONEYS** ively. All such fines, penalties and license moneys shall be appropriated exclusively to the use and support of common schools in the respective subdivisions where the same may accrue.

SEC. 6. The legislature shall provide for the free instruction in common schools of this State, of all persons between the ages of five and twenty-one years.

SEC. 7. Provisions shall be made by general law for an equitable distribution of the income of the fund set apart for the support of the common schools, among the several school distr cts of the State, and no appropriation shall be made from said fund to any district for the year in which school is not maintained at least three months.

SEC. 8. University, agricultural college, common school, or other lands, which are now held, or may hereafter be acquired by the State for educational purposes, shall not be sold for less than seven dollars per acre, nor less than the appraised value.

SEC. 9. All funds belonging to the State for educational purposes, the interest and income whereof only are to be used, shall be deemed trust funds held by the State, **FUNDS TO RE-** and the State shall supply all losses thereof that **MAIN** may in any manner accrue, so that the same shall **INVIO-** remain forever inviolate and undiminished; and **LATE.** shall not be invested or loaned except on United States or state securities, or registered county bonds of this State; and such funds, with the interest and income thereof, are hereby solemnly pledged for the purposes for which they are granted and set apart, and shall not be transferred to any other fund for other uses.

SEC. 10. The general government of the university of Nebraska shall, under the direction of the legislature, be vested in a board of six regents, to be styled the **GOV-** board of regents of the university of Nebraska, **ERN-** who shall be elected by the electors of the State at **MENT** large, and their term of office, except those chosen **OF UNI-** at the first election, as hereinafter provided, shall **VER-** be six years. Their duties and powers shall be pre- **SITY.** scribed by law; and they shall receive no compensation, but may be reimbursed their actual expenses incurred in the discharge of their duties.

SEC. 11. No sectarian instruction shall be allowed in any school or institution supported in whole or in part by the public funds set apart for educational purposes; nor shall the State accept any grant, conveyance, or bequest of money, lands or other property, to be used for sectarian purposes.

SEC. 12. The legislature may provide by law for the establishment of a school or schools for the safe keeping, education, employment, and reformation of all children under the age of sixteen years, who, for want of proper parental care, or other cause, are growing up in mendicancy or crime.

ARTICLE IX.—REVENUE AND FINANCE.

SECTION 1. The legislature shall provide such revenue as may be needful, by levying a tax by valuation, so that every person or corporation shall pay a tax in proportion to the value of his, her, or its property and franchises, the value to be ascertained in such manner as the legislature **MINOR TAXES.** shall direct, and it shall have power to tax peddlers, auctioneers, brokers, hawkers, commission merchants, showmen, jugglers, inn-keepers, liquor dealers, toll bridges, ferries, insurance, telegraph and express interests or business, venders of patents, in such manner as it shall direct by general law, uniform as to the class upon which it operates.

SEC. 2. The property of the State, counties and municipal corporations, both real and personal, shall be exempt from taxation, and such other property as may be used exclusively for agricultural and horticultural societies, for school, religious, cemetery and charitable purposes, may **LANDS EX-** be exempted from taxation, but such exemptions **EMPTED** shall be only by general law. In the assessment of **FROM TAXA-** all real estate encumbered by public easement, any **TION.** depreciation occasioned by such easement may be deducted in the valuation of such property. The legislature may provide that the increased value of lands, by reason of live fences, fruit and forest trees grown and cultivated thereon, shall not be taken into account in the assessment thereof.

SEC. 3. The right of redemption from all sales of real estate, for the non-payment of taxes or special assessments of any character whatever, shall exist in favor of owners and persons interested in such real estate for a period of not less than two years from such sales thereof; *Provided*, That occupants shall in all cases be served with personal notice before the time of redemption expires.

SEC. 4. The legislature shall have no power to release or discharge any county, city, township, town, or district whatever, or the inhabitants thereof, or any corporation, or the property therein, from their or its proportionate share of taxes to be levied for state purposes, or due any municipal corporation, nor shall commutation for such taxes be authorized in any form whatever.

SEC. 5. County authorities shall never assess taxes the

aggregate of which shall exceed one and a half dollars per hundred dollars valuation, except for the payment of indebtedness existing at the adoption of this constitution, unless authorized by a vote of the people of the county.

SEC. 6. The legislature may vest the corporate authorities of cities, towns, and villages, with power to make local improvements by special assessments, or by special taxation of property benefited. For all other corporate purposes, all municipal corporations may be vested with authority to assess and collect taxes, but such taxes shall be uniform in respect to persons and property within the jurisdiction of the body imposing the same.

SEC. 7. Private property shall not be liable to be taken or sold for the payment of the corporate debts of municipal corporations. The legislature shall not impose taxes upon municipal corporations, or the inhabitants or property thereof, for corporate purposes.

SEC. 8. The legislature at its first session shall provide by law for the funding of all outstanding warrants and other indebtedness of the state, at a rate of interest not exceeding eight per cent per annum.

SEC. 9. The legislature shall provide by law that all claims upon the treasury shall be examined and adjusted by the auditor and approved by the secretary of state before any warrant for the amount allowed shall be drawn; *Provided,* That a party aggrieved by the decision of the auditor and secretary of state may appeal to [the] district court.

ARTICLE [X.]—COUNTIES.

SECTION 1. No new county shall be formed or established by the legislature which will reduce the county or counties, or either of them, to a less area than four hundred square miles, nor shall any county be formed of a less area.

SEC. 2. No county shall be divided, or have any part stricken therefrom without first submitting the question to a vote of the people of the county, nor unless a majority of all the legal voters of the county voting on the question shall vote for the same.

SEC. 3. There shall be no territory stricken from any organized county unless a majority of the voters living in such territory shall petition for such division, and no territory shall be added to any organized county without the consent of the majority of the voters of the county to which it is proposed to be added; but the portion so stricken off and added to another county, or formed in whole or in part into a new county, shall be holden for and obliged to pay its proportion of the indebtedness of the counties from which it has been taken.

SEC. 4. The legislature shall provide by law for the election of such county and township officers as may be necessary.

SEC. 5. The legislature shall provide by general law for township organization, under which any county may organize whenever a majority of the legal voters of such county, voting at any general election, shall so determine; and in any county that shall have adopted a township organization, the question of continuing the same may be submitted to a vote of the electors of such county at a general election in the manner that shall be provided by law.

ARTICLE [XI.]—RAILROAD CORPORATIONS.

SECTION 1. Every railroad corporation organized or doing business in this State, under the laws or authority thereof, or of any other state, or of the United States, shall have and **RAIL-ROAD COR-PORA-TIONS.** maintain a public office or place in this State for the transaction of its business, where transfers of stock shall be made, and in which shall be kept, for public inspection, books in which shall be recorded the amount of capital stock subscribed, and by whom, the names of the owners of its stock, and the amounts owned by them respectively, the amount of stock paid in and by whom, the transfers of said stock, the amount of its assets and liabilities, and the names and places of residence of its officers. The directors of every railroad corporation, or other parties having control of its road, shall annually make a report, under oath, to the auditor of public accounts, or some officer to be designated by law, of the amount received from passengers and freight, and such other matters relating to railroads as may be prescribed by law. And the legislature shall pass laws enforcing by suitable penalties the provisions of this section.

SEC. 2. The rolling stock and all other movable property belonging to any railroad company or corporation in this State shall be liable to execution and sale in the same manner as the personal property of individuals, and the legislature shall pass no law exempting any such property from execution and sale.

SEC. 3. No railroad corporation or telegraph company shall consolidate its stock, property, franchises, or earnings, in whole or in part, with any other railroad corporation or telegraph company owning a parallel or competing line; and in no case shall any consolidation take place except upon public notice of at least sixty days to all stockholders in such manner as may be provided by law.

SEC. 4. Railways heretofore constructed or that may hereafter be constructed in this State, are hereby declared public highways, and shall be free to all persons for the transportation of their persons and property thereon, under such regulations as may be prescribed by law. And the legislature may from time to time pass laws establishing reasonable maximum rates of charges for the transportation of passengers and freight on the different railroads in this State. The liability of railroad corporations as common carriers shall never be limited.

SEC. 5. No railroad corporation shall issue any stock or bonds except for money, labor, or property actually received and applied to the purposes for which such corporation was created, and all stock, dividends, and other fictitious increase of the capital stock or indebtedness of any such corporation shall be void. The capital stock of railway corporations shall not be increased for any purpose, except after public notice for sixty days, in such manner as may be provided by law.

SEC. 6. The exercise of the power and the right of eminent domain shall never be so construed or abridged as to prevent the taking, by the legislature, of the property and franchises of incorporated companies already organized or hereafter to be organized, and subjecting them to the public necessity, the same as individuals.

SEC. 7. The legislature shall pass laws to correct abuses, and prevent unjust discrimination and extortion in all charges of express, telegraph, and railroad companies in this State, and enforce such laws by adequate penalties to the extent, if necessary for that purpose, of forfeiture of their property and franchises.

SEC. 8. No railroad corporation, organized under the laws of any other state, or of the United States, and doing business in this State, shall be entitled to exercise the right of eminent domain, or have power to acquire the right of way, or real estate for depot or other uses, until it shall have become a body corporate pursuant to and in accordance with the laws of this State.

ARTICLE [XII.]—MUNICIPAL CORPORATIONS.

SECTION 1. No city, county, town, precinct, municipality, or other subdivision of the State, shall ever become a subscriber to the capital stock, or owner of such stock, or any portion of interest therein, of any railroad or private corporation, or association.

ARTICLE [XIII.]—MISCELLANEOUS CORPORATIONS.

SECTION 1. No corporation shall be created by special law, nor its charter extended, changed, or amended, except those for charitable, educational, penal, or reformatory purposes, which are to be and remain under the patronage and control of the State, but the legislature shall provide by general laws for the organizations of all corporations hereafter to be created. All general laws passed pursuant to this section may be altered from time to time, or repealed.

SEC. 2. No such general law shall be passed by the legislature granting the right to construct and operate a street railroad within any city, town, or incorporated village, without first requiring the consent of a majority of the electors thereof.

SEC. 3. All corporations may sue and be sued in like cases as natural persons.

SEC. 4. In all cases of claims against corporations and joint stock associations, the exact amount justly due shall be first ascertained, and after the corporate property shall have been exhausted, the original subscribers thereof shall be individually liable to the extent of their unpaid subscription, and the liability for the unpaid subscription shall follow the stock.

SEC. 5. The legislature shall provide by law that in all elections for directors or managers of incorporated companies every stockholder shall [have] the right to vote in person or proxy for the number of shares of stock owned by him, for as many persons as there are directors or managers to be elected, or to cumulate said shares and give one candidate as many votes as the number of directors multiplied by the number of his shares of stock shall equal, or to distribute them upon the same principle among as many candidates as he shall think fit; and such directors or managers shall not be elected in any other manner.

SEC. 6. All existing charters or grants of special or exclusive privileges under which organization shall not have taken place, or which shall not be in operation within sixty days from the time this constitution takes effect, shall thereafter have no validity or effect whatever.

SEC. 7. Every stockholder in a banking corporation or institution shall be individually responsible and liable to its creditors, over and above the amount of stock by him held, to an amount equal to his respective stock or shares so held, for all its liabilities accruing while he remains such stockholder; and all banking corporations shall publish quarterly statements, under oath, of their assets and liabilities.

ARTICLE [XIV.]—STATE, COUNTY, AND MUNICIPAL INDEBTEDNESS.

SECTION 1. The State may, to meet casual deficits or failures in the revenues, contract debts never to exceed in the aggregate one hundred thousand dollars; and no greater indebtedness **BONDS OF THE STATE.** shall be incurred except for purpose of repelling invasion, suppressing insurrection, or defending the State in war; and provision shall be made for the payment of the interest annually, as it shall accrue, by a tax levied for the purpose, or from other sources of revenue, which law providing for the payment of such interest by such tax shall be irrepealable until such debt be paid.

SEC. 2. No city, county, town, precinct, municipality

or other subdivision of the State, shall ever make donations to any railroad or other works of internal improvement, unless a proposition so to do shall have been first submitted to the qualified electors thereof at an election by authority of law; *Provided,* That such donations of a county with the donations of such subdivisions in the aggregate shall not exceed ten per cent of the assessed valuation of such county; *Provided further,* That any city or county may, by a two-thirds vote, increase such indebtedness five per cent in addition to such ten per cent, and no bonds or evidences of indebtedness so issued shall be valid unless the same shall have endorsed thereon a certificate signed by the secretary and auditor of state, showing that the same is issued pursuant to law.

MUNICIPAL HELP FOR RAILROADS.

SEC. 3. The credit of the State shall never be given or loaned in aid of any individual, association, or corporation.

ARTICLE [XV.]—MILITIA.

SECTION 1. The legislature shall determine what persons shall constitute the militia of the State, and may provide for organizing and disciplining the same.

ARTICLE [XVI.]—MISCELLANEOUS PROVISIONS.

SECTION 1. Executive and judicial officers and members of the legislature, before they enter upon their official duties, shall take and subscribe the following oath or affirmation: " I do solemnly swear (or affirm) that I will support the constitution of the United States and the constitution of the State of Nebraska, and will faithfully discharge the duties of ———— according to the best of my ability, and that at the election at which I was chosen to fill said office I have not improperly influenced in any way the vote of any elector, and have not accepted, nor will I accept or receive, directly or indirectly, any money or other valuable thing from any corporation, company, or person, or any promise of office for any official act or influence (for any vote I may give or withhold on any bill, resolution, or appropriation.)" Any such officer, or member of the legislature who shall refuse to take the oath herein prescribed, shall forfeit his office, and any person who shall be convicted of having sworn falsely to, or of violating his said oath, shall forfeit his office, and thereafter be disqualified from holding any office of profit or trust in this State, unless he shall have been restored to civil rights.

SEC. 2. Any person who is in default as collector and custodian of public money or property, shall not be eligible to any office of trust or profit under the constitution or laws of this State; nor shall any person convicted of felony be eligible to office unless he shall have been restored to civil rights.

SEC. 3. Drunkenness shall be cause of impeachment and removal from office.

ARTICLE [XVII.]—AMENDMENTS.

SECTION 1. Either branch of the legislature may propose amendments to this constitution, and if the same be agreed to by three-fifths of the members elected to each house, such proposed amendments shall be entered on the journals, with the yeas and nays, and published at least once each week in at least one newspaper in each county, where a newspaper is published, for three months immediately preceding the next election of senators and representatives, at which election the same shall be submitted to the electors for approval or rejection, and if a majority of the electors voting at such election adopt such amendments, the same shall become a part of this constitution. When more than one amendment is submitted at the same election, they shall be so submitted as to enable the electors to vote on each amendment separately.

SEC. 2. When three-fifths of the members elected to each branch of the legislature deem it necessary to call a convention to revise, amend, or change this constitution, **CONVENTION TO REVISE CONSTITUTION.** they shall recommend to the electors to vote at the next election of members of the legislature for or against a convention; and if a majority voting at said election vote for a convention, the legislature shall, at its next session, provide by law for calling the same. The convention shall consist of as many members as the house of representatives, who shall be chosen in the same manner, and shall meet within three months after their election for the purpose aforesaid. No amendment or change of this constitution, agreed upon by such convention, shall take effect until the same has been submitted to the electors of the State, and adopted by a majority of those voting for and against the same.

ARTICLE [XVIII.]—SCHEDULE.

SECTION 1. That no inconvenience may arise from the revisions and changes made in the constitution of this State, and to carry the same into effect, it is hereby ordained and declared that all laws in force at the time of the adoption of this constitution, not inconsistent therewith, and all rights, actions, prosecutions, claims, and contracts of this State, individuals or bodies corporate, shall continue to be as valid as if this constitution had not been adopted.

SEC. 2. All fines, taxes, penalties, and forfeitures owing to the State of Nebraska, or to the people thereof, under the present constitution and laws, shall inure to the use of the people of the State of Nebraska, under this constitution.

SEC. 3. Recognizances, bonds, obligations, and all other

instruments entered into or executed upon the adoption of this constitution, to the people of the State of Nebraska, to the State of Nebraska, to any state or county officer, or public body, shall remain binding and valid, and rights and liabilities upon the same shall continue: and all crimes and misdemeanors shall be tried and punished as though no change had been made in the constitution of this State.

SEC. 4. All existing courts which are not in this constitution specifically enumerated, and concerning which no other provision is herein made, shall continue in existence, and exercise their present jurisdiction until otherwise provided by law.

SEC. 5. All persons now filling any office or appointment shall continue in the exercise of the duties thereof, according to their respective commissions, elections, or appointments, unless by this constitution it is otherwise directed.

SEC. 6. The district attorneys now in office shall continue during their unexpired terms to hold and exercise the duties of their respective offices in the judicial districts herein created, in which they severally reside. In each of the remaining districts one such officer shall be elected at the first general election, and hold his office until the expiration of the terms of those now in office.

SEC. 7. This constitution shall be submitted to the people of the State of Nebraska, for adoption or rejection, at an election to be held on the second Tuesday of October, A.D., 1875, and there shall be separately submitted at the same time, for adoption or rejection, the independent article relating to "Seat of government," and the independent article "Allowing electors to express their preference for United States senator."

SEC. 8. At said election the qualified electors shall vote at the usual places of voting, and the said election shall be conducted and the returns thereof made according to the laws now in force regulating general elections, except as herein otherwise provided.

SEC. 9. The secretary of state shall, at least twenty days before said election, cause to be delivered to the county clerk of each county, blank poll-books, tally lists, and forms of returns, and twice as many of properly prepared printed ballots for the said election as there are voters in such county, the expense whereof shall be audited and paid as other public printing ordered by the secretary as is by law required to be audited and paid; and the several county clerks shall, at least five days before said election, cause to be distributed to the judges of election, in each election precinct in their respective counties, said blank poll-books, tally lists, forms of return, and tickets.

SEC. 10. At the said election the ballots shall be of the following form:

For the new constitution.

Against the new constitution.

For the article relating to "Seat of government."

Against the article relating to "Seat of government."

For the article "Allowing electors to express their preference for United States senators."

Against the article "Allowing the electors to express their preference for United States senators."

SEC. 11. The returns of the whole vote cast, and of the votes for the adoption or rejection of this constitution, and for or against the articles respectfully submitted shall be made by the several county clerks to the secretary of state, within fourteen days after the election, and the returns of the said vote shall within three days thereafter, be examined and canvassed by the president of this convention, the secretary of state, and the governor, or any two of them, and proclamation shall be made forthwith by the governor, or the president of this convention, of the result of the canvass.

SEC. 12. If it shall appear that a majority of the votes polled are "for the new constitution," then so much of this new constitution as was not separately submitted to be voted on by article shall be the supreme law of the State of Nebraska, on and after the first day of November, A.D. 1875. But if it shall appear that a majority of the votes polled were "against the new constitution," the whole thereof, including the articles separately submitted, shall be null and void. If the votes "for the new constitution" shall adopt the same, and it shall appear that a majority of the votes polled are for the article relating to the "seat of government," said article shall be a part of the constitution of this State. If the votes "for the new constitution" shall adopt the same and it shall appear that the majority of the votes polled are for the article "allowing electors to express their preference for United States senator," said article shall be a part of the constitution of this State.

SEC. 13. The general election of this State shall be held on the Tuesday succeeding the first Monday of November of each year. All state, district, county, precinct, and township officers, by the constitution or laws made elective by the people, except school district officers and municipal officers in cities, villages, and towns, shall be elected at a general election to be held as aforesaid. Judges of the supreme, district, and county courts, all elective county and precinct officers, and all other elective officers, the time for the election of whom is not herein otherwise provided for, and which are not included in the above exception, shall be elected at the first general election, and thereafter at the general election next preceding the time of the termination of their respective terms of office; *Provided*, That the office of no county commissioner shall be vacated hereby.

SEC. 14. The terms of office of all state and county officers, or judges of the supreme, district and county courts, and regents of the university shall begin on the first Thursday after the first Tuesday in January next succeeding their election. The present state and county officers, members of the legislature, and regents of the university, shall continue in office until their successors shall be elected and qualified.

TERMS OF OFFICE.

SEC. 15. The supreme, district, and county courts established by this constitution shall be the successors respectively of the supreme court, the district courts, and the probate courts, having jurisdiction under the existing constitution.

SEC. 16. The supreme, district, and probate courts now in existence shall continue, and the judges thereof shall exercise the power and retain their present jurisdiction until the courts provided for by this constitution shall be organized.

SEC. 17. All cases, matters, and proceedings pending and undetermined in the several courts, and all records, judgments, orders, and decrees remaining therein, are hereby transferred to and shall be proceeded and enforced in and by the successors thereof respectively.

SEC. 18. If this constitution be adopted, the existing constitution shall cease in all its provisions on the first day of November, A.D. 1875.

SEC. 19. The provisions of this constitution required to be executed prior to the adoption or rejection thereof shall take effect and be in force immediately.

SEC. 20. The legislature shall pass all laws necessary to carry into effect the provisions of this constitution.

SEC. 21. On the taking effect of this constitution, all state officers hereby continued in office shall, before proceeding in the further discharge of their duties, take an oath or affirmation to support this constitution.

SEC. 22. The regents of the university shall be elected at the first general election under this constitution, and be classified by lot so that two shall hold their offices for the term of two years, two for the term of four years, and two for the term of six years.

SEC. 23. The present executive state officers shall continue in office until the executive state officers provided for in this constitution shall be elected and qualified.

SEC. 24. The returns of the whole vote cast for the judges of the supreme and district courts, district attorneys, and regents of the university, under the first general election, shall be made by the several county clerks to the secretary of state within fourteen days after the election; and the returns of the said votes shall, within three days thereafter, be examined and canvassed by the governor, secretary of state, and the president of this convention, or any two of them, and certificates of election shall forthwith be issued by the secretary of state to the persons found to be elected.

SEC. 25. The auditor shall draw the warrants of the State quarterly for the payment of the salaries of all officers under this constitution, whose compensation is not otherwise provided for, which shall be paid out of any funds not otherwise appropriated.

SEC. 26. Until otherwise provided by law, the judges of the district court shall fix the time of holding courts in their respective districts.

SEC. 27. The members of the first legislature under this constitution shall be elected in the year 1876.

SEC. 28. This constitution shall be enrolled and deposited in the office of the secretary of state, and printed copies thereof shall be prefixed to the books containing the laws of the State, and all future editions thereof.

PROPOSITIONS SEPARATELY SUBMITTED.

ALLOWING ELECTORS TO EXPRESS THEIR PREFERENCE FOR UNITED STATES SENATORS.

The legislature may provide that at the general election immediately preceding the expiration of a term of a United States senator from this State, the electors may by ballot, express their preference for some person for the office of United States senator. The votes cast for such candidates shall be canvassed and returned in the same manner as for state officers.

SEAT OF GOVERNMENT.

The seat of government of the State shall not be removed or re-located without the assent of a majority of the electors of the State, voting thereupon at a general election or elections, under such rules and regulations as to the number of elections and manner of voting, and places to be voted for, as may be prescribed by law; *Provided*, The question of removal may be submitted at such other general elections as may be provided by law.

Done in convention at Lincoln, June 12, 1875.

J. L. WEBSTER, President of Convention,

GUY A. BROWN, Secretary.

INDEX.

NEW PUBLICATIONS.

Elementary Botanical Exercises.
    By CHARLES E. BESSEY, Ph.D. This is a simple outline of field work in botany for one year, with each month's work indicated. Price, post-paid ....$ .30

Questions on the Art of Shakespeare.
    By L. A. SHERMAN, Ph.D. Hamlet, Macbeth, and others. Paper, price each .... .10

History and Civil Government of Nebraska.
    By J. A. BARRETT, A.M. Price, post-paid.... .65

Outline Map of Nebraska.
    For school use, 11x22. Price. 3c each, or per 100, 2.00

Moral Instruction in Public Schools.
    An address by E. E. WHITE, Ph.D. Price, 5c, or per 100.. 2.00

The North-Western Journal of Education.
    Monthly, except August, per year.................... 1.25

J. H. MILLER, Publisher,
Lincoln, Neb.

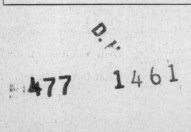